TALKING TURKEY

TALKING TURKEY

A Food Lover's Guide to the Origins of Culinary Words and Phrases

ROBERT HENDRICKSON

Skyhorse Publishing

Skyhorse Publishing books may be purchased in bulk at special discounts for sales promotion, corporate gifts, fund-raising, or educational purposes. Special editions can also be created to specifications. For details, contact the Special Sales Department, Skyhorse Publishing, 307 West 36th Street, 11th Floor, New York, NY 10018 or info@skyhorsepublishing.com.

Skyhorse® and Skyhorse Publishing® are registered trademarks of Skyhorse Publishing, Inc.®, a Delaware corporation.

Visit out website at www.skyhorsepublishing.com.

10 9 8 7 6 5 4 3 2 1

Library of Congress Cataloging-in-Publication Data is available on file

ISBN: 978-1-62636-550-6

Printed in China

EDITOR'S NOTE

Food is a favorite topic of conversation around the world—how to create it, how to season it, how to compliment it with other foods, how to serve it . . . the list goes on. Yet little attention is paid to where the names of food come from or why so many of our daily phrases involve food, whether or not they actually relate to the kitchen. Fortunately, this delightful phrasebook is here to bring some foodie history to the table!

"Bring home the bacon," "couch potato," "in a pickle" . . . all phrases we use regularly, at home, with our friends, about ourselves, but where do they come from? *Talking Turkey* is here with the etymology of each phrase, meticulously going through historical facts before presenting it in a few concise words. Go on, flip through—you're guaranteed to find some surprises!

A

acknowledge the corn. Much used in the 19th century as a synonym for our "copping a plea," this phrase is said to have arisen when a man was arrested and charged with stealing four horses and the corn (grain) to feed them. "I acknowledge [admit to] the corn," he declared.

acorn. *Acorn* is an ancient word deriving from the Old English aecern, meaning "fruit" or "berry." Its present form acorn is due in large part to folk etymology; people believed that the word aecern was made up of "oak" and "corn" because the fruit came from the oak and was a corn or seed of that tree. Thus aecern came to be pronounced and spelled "acorn."

Adam's apple. Adam never ate an apple, at least not in the biblical account of his transgressions, which refers only to unspecified forbidden fruit on the tree in the Garden of Eden. The forbidden fruit of which the Lord said "Ye shall not eat of the fruit which is in the midst of the garden, neither shall ye touch it, lest ye die" (Gen. 3:3) was probably an apricot or pomegranate, and the Muslims—intending no joke—believe it was a banana. Many fruits and vegetables have been called apples. Even in medieval times, pomegranates were "apples of Carthage"; dates, "finger apples"; and potatoes, "apples of the earth." At any rate, tradition has it that Adam succumbed to Eve's wiles and ate of an apple from which she took the first bite, that a piece stuck in his throat forming the lump we call the *Adam's apple*, and that all of us, particularly males, inherited this mark of his "fall." Modern scientific physiology, as opposed to folk anatomy, explains this projection of the neck, most prominent in adolescents, as being anterior thyroid cartilage of the larynx. But pioneer anatomists honored the superstition in the mid-18th century by calling it *pomum Adami*, or *Adam's apple*. They simply could find no other explanation for this evasive lump in the throat that even seemed to move up and down.

agave. Any of several southwestern plants with tough, spiny, sword-shaped leaves. Named for Agave, daughter of the legendary Cadmus, who introduced the Greek alphabet, the large *Agave* genus includes the remarkable century plant *(Agave americana)*, which blooms once and dies (though anytime after 15 years, not after 100 years, as was once believed). Introduced to Europe from America in the 16th century, this big agave is often used there for fences. It is regarded as a religious charm by pilgrims to Mecca, who hang a leaf of it over their doors to ward off evil spirits and indicate that they have made the pilgrimage.

Albany beef. Sturgeon was once so plentiful in New York's Hudson River that it was humorously called *Albany beef*. The term is first recorded in 1791 and was in use through the 19th century; sturgeon caviar was so cheap in those days that it was part of the free lunch served in bars. Cod was similarly called *Cape Cod turkey* in Massachusetts.

alcohol. One apocryphal tale claims that an Arab named Jabir ibn Hazzan "invented" alcohol in about A.D. 800 when he discovered the process of distilling wine. In trying to find the intoxicating agent in wine he distilled *alkuhl*, which meant "a finely refined spirit." According to the story, the word itself was adopted from the name for an antimony powder used at the time as an eyelid cosmetic (an ancient eye shadow). More sober etymologists will only say that alcohol derives from the Arabic *alkuhl*, powdered antimony, or the distillate.

all foreign fruit, plants are free from duty. This is the classic example of the importance of proper punctuation. In the 1890s a congressional clerk transcribing a new law was supposed to write: "All foreign fruit-plants are free from duty" but changed the hyphen to a comma and wrote: "All foreign fruit, plants are free from duty." Before Congress could amend his error, the government lost over $2 million in taxes.

all hands and the cook. *All hands and the cook on deck!* was a cry probably first heard on New England whalers in the early 19th century when everyone aboard was called topside to cut in on a whale, work that had to be done quickly. Fishermen also used the expression, and still do, and it had currency among American cowboys to indicate a dangerous situation—when, for example, even the cook was needed to keep the herd under control.

all hat and no cattle. A Texan phrase describing someone who acts rich or important but has no substance, such as a person who pretends to be a cattle baron, even dressing the part: "He's all hat and no cattle."

all that meat and no potatoes. An exclamation of plea sure and admiration by a man on seeing a woman with an attractive figure, although the term and/or the exclamation might be offensive to many women. *See* POTATO; MEAT AND POTATOES; HOT POTATO.

all the tea in China. All the tea in China would be nearly 600,000 tons, according to the 1985 estimates of the United States Department of Agriculture. It may be an Americanism, but this expression denoting a great sum probably is of British origin and over a century old; the trouble is that no one has been able to authoritatively pin it down.

almond; Jordan almond. Almonds, which came out of China, are today the most popular of all nuts worldwide. They especially please the Japanese, who often have English signs reading "Almond" outside shops that would otherwise say "Bakery" or "Confectionery" in their own language. But then this ancient nut (mentioned 73 times in the Old Testament) has been associated with beauty and virility for centuries. Rich in protein, amino acids, magnesium, iron, calcium, and phosphorus, and a good source of vitamins B and E, the almond is also a harbinger of spring and the joyous expectancy of new life and love; in fact, the tree's pale pink blossoms appear about the time that the swallows return to Capistrano. The word *almond* has its roots in *amandola*, the medieval Latin word for the nut. Jordan almonds come from Spain; they have no connection with the country named Jordan, as many people assume. The term "Jordan almond" is simply a corruption of the French *jardin amande*, which translates as "garden almond."

anadama bread. Anadama bread, a Yankee cornmeal recipe, offers one of the most humorous stories connected with any foodstuff . Tradition has it that a Yankee farmer or fisherman, whose wife Anna was too lazy to cook for him, concocted the recipe. On tasting the result of his efforts a neighbor asked him what he called the bread, the crusty

Yankee replying, "Anna, damn her!" Another version claims that the husband was a Yankee sea captain who endearingly referred to his wife as "Anna, damn 'er." Anna's bread was much loved by his crew because it was delicious and would not spoil on long sea voyages. The captain is said to have written the following epitaph for his wife: "Anna was a lovely bride,/but Anna, damn'er, up and died."

an apple a day keeps the doctor away. A proverb that dates back to the early 19th century, states *Bartlett's*. An apple a day is nutritious and delicious but doesn't provide any immunity against illness, according to the latest scientific studies.

anchovy. A small herring like fish, widely used as an appetizer. The word's origin is unknown.

apple of discord. This legendary golden apple was thrown on the table by the god Eris (Discord) at the wedding of Thetis and Peleus, to which all the Greek gods but Eris had been invited. The apple was said to be "for the most beautiful woman" present, and Paris judged between Hera (Juno), Aphrodite (Venus), and Athene (Minerva), who offered him, respectively, bribes of power, sex, and martial glory. He chose Aphrodite, and the vengeance of Hera and Athene supposedly led to the fall of Troy. The *apple of discord* still means the cause of a dispute, or something to be disputed.

apple-polisher. The traditional practice of a student giving teacher a bright, shiny apple is the source for this expression for a sycophant, the Americanism being first recorded in 1928. The synonym sycophant interestingly has its origins in another fruit, figs.

apple; apple hawk; apple orchard. *Apple* for a baseball dates back to the early 1920s; before that the ball had been called a "pea," a term heard no more. A good fielder was called an *apple hawk* at the time, this term obsolete now, and the ball park was called an *apple orchard*, an expression still occasionally used. *Apple* itself comes from the Old English *appel* for the fruit. An *apple* can also be a derogatory name given to certain American Indians by other American Indians who believe their values are too much like those of whites; that is, they are, like an apple, red on the outside and white on the inside. This term is based on the American black derisive name *Oreo* for a black person whose values are believed to be too much like those of whites. An Oreo is a trademarked chocolate cookie with creamy white filling.

apple-knocker. An abusive term meaning a stupid person, especially a rustic stupid person, that is still used by city dwellers. The term is recorded in this sense in a 1939 *New Yorker* story: "I had a reform-school technique, whereas them other sailors was apple-knockers. They were so dumb they couldn't find their nose with both hands." *Apple-knocker* first meant a fruit picker, deriving from the mistaken urban belief that fruit is harvested by being knocked from trees with long sticks.

the apple never falls far from the tree. Children always share the characteristics of their parents. The mid-19th-century proverb is usually said in a negative sense, emphasizing bad characteristics.

apple of one's eye. That which one holds dearest, as in "You're the apple of my eye." The phrase is from the Bible (Deut. 32:10), which says the Lord kept Israel "as the apple of his eye." *Pupillam*, or pupil, is actually the Latin for the "apple" of the phrase, but English translators of the Bible used "apple" because this was the early word for the pupil of the eye, which was thought to be a solid apple-shaped body. Because it is essential to sight, the eye's apple, or pupil, is to be cherished and protected, and the *apple of one's eye* came to mean anything extremely precious. The literal translation of the Hebrew phrase, incidentally, is "You are as the little man in the eye" (one's own reflection in the pupil of another's eye).

apple pandowdy. Imogene Wolcott's *New England Yankee Cookbook* (1939) gives several authentic recipes for this deep-dish apple dessert, noting that the modern version is often called apple brown Betty. It has also been called *flummery apple pot-pie, apple Jonathan, apple Johnny,* and *apple slump.* So much did Harriet Beecher Stowe like the dish that she named her Concord, Massachusetts, house Apple Slump in its honor.

apple-pie order. One old story holds that New England house wives were so meticulous and tidy when making their apple pies—carefully cutting thin slices of apples, methodically arranging them in rows inside the pie, making sure that the pinches joining the top and bottom crusts were perfectly even, etc.—that the expression *apple-pie order* arose for prim and precise orderliness. A variant on the yarn has an early American house wife baking seven pies every Monday and arranging them neatly on shelves, one for every day of the week in strict order. Nice stories, but the term *apple-pie* order is probably British in origin, dating back to at least the early 17th century. It may be a corruption of the French *nappes-pliées,* folded linen (neatly folded) or cap-a-pie, "from head to foot." Yet no use of either *nappes-pliées* order or cap-a-pie order appears in English. "Alpha beta order" has also been suggested, but seems unlikely. The true source of the term must still be considered a mystery, the matter far from in apple-pie order.

apple slump. Apple slump, a popular New England dessert, takes on another meaning in Louisa May Alcott's story "Transcendental Wild Oats" (1876), an account of her father Bronson Alcott's failed utopian community, Fruitlands, 32 years earlier: "'Poor Fruitlands! The name was as great a failure as the rest!' continued Abel [Bronson Alcott], with a sigh, as a frostbitten apple fell from a leafless bough at his feet. But the sigh changed to a smile as his wife added, in a half-tender, half-satirical tone, 'Don't you think Apple Slump would be a better name for it, dear?'" The dessert is sometimes called *apple pandowdy* and *flummery*. So much did Harriet Beecher Stowe like the dish that she named her Concord, Massachusetts, house Apple Slump.

apples of perpetual youth. These were golden apples of Scandinavian mythology that were in the care of Idhunn, daughter of Svald the dwarf. By eating them, the gods preserved their youth.

apricot. The Romans called this fruit *praecoquum*, or "early ripe." From there the word entered Arabic as *alburquq* and went into Portuguese as *albricoque*, whence it come into English as *apricock*. By the 18th century the shears of prudery had pruned the word from *apricock* to *apricot*.

Arizona strawberries. American cowboys and lumberjacks used this term as a humorous synonym for beans, also employing the variations *Arkansas strawberries*,

Mexican strawberries, and *prairie strawberries*. Dried beans were pink in color like strawberries. One wit noted that the only way these beans could be digested was for the consumer to break wild horses.

arroz con pollo. A Mexican chicken and rice dish seasoned with garlic, saffron, paprika, and other spices that was first introduced to the United States in the Southwest but is now known throughout the country. The Spanish name translates simply as "rice with chicken."

artichoke; Jerusalem artichoke. As the poet Richard Armour observed, the *artichoke* is the one vegetable you have more of when you finish eating it, due to its compact leaves, which are scraped with the teeth and discarded. Often called the *globe* or *French artichoke*, it is the flower bud of a thistle picked before it blooms. At one time it was seriously suggested that the plant was so named because some *artist* had *choked* on the inedible "needles" covering its delicious base, or "heart." Actually *artichoke* has more prosaic and complicated origins. The Arabians called it *al* ("the") *kharshuf*, which became *alcachofa* in Spanish. Northern Italians corrupted the Spanish version to *articiocco* and this entered French as *artichaut*, from which our *artichoke* evolved. It is true that the English *choke* in the word replacing the French *chaut* may have been influenced by the sensation one gets from eating the wrong part of the vegetable. As for the *Jerusalem artichoke*, it neither comes from Jerusalem, is an artichoke, nor tastes anything like an artichoke. The starchy underground tuber (a good potato substitute) was called *girasole articiocco*, "sunflower artichoke," by northern Italians because it is a member of the sunflower family and resembles a sunflower in leaf and stem. To Englishmen the word *girasole* sounded like *Jerusalem*, and they mistakenly translated the name as *Jerusalem artichoke*.

as different as chalk and cheese. A phrase dating back to Middle English that shows the great difference between two things, as in "It's chalk and cheese."

asparagus. There is a story that asparagus takes its name from the Greek *aspharagos*, meaning according to this theory, "as long as one's throat," because diners often swallowed the spears whole. But the meaning of the word *aspharagos* from which our *asparagus* derives is unclear and more likely meant "sprout or shoot" in Greek.

The great chef Brillat-Savarin told of a giant asparagus stalk growing in an Episcopal bishop's garden, so immense that it became the talk of the town as it rose from the ground. Only when the bishop went out to cut the tempting stalk did he learn that it wasn't real but a perfect imitation made by a local canon, "who had carved a wooden asparagus . . . had stuck it by stealth into the bed, and lifted it a little every day to imitate the natural growth."

Some old-timers still call asparagus *grass*, from the homily expression "sparrowgrass" commonly used as a name for the vegetable over the last three centuries. The Romans cultivated the vegetable as early as 200 B.C., growing some stalks at Ravenna that weighed a full three pounds and gathering stems in the Getulia plains of Africa that were actually 12 feet tall.

There is an interesting true story about blanched white asparagus. According to a *New York Times* correspondent, at a recent dinner party "a certain guest complimented the German hostess and said: 'This white asparagus is as beautiful as a naked woman,' becoming the first asparagus eater to have noticed a resemblance between asparagus and the attributes of the female sex." *See* QUICKER THAN YOU CAN COOK ASPARAGUS.

as sure as God made little green apples. Very certain, as in "He'll be there as sure as God made little green apples." First recorded in the mid-19th century, the phrase is sometimes heard with the word *green* deleted.

aubergine. Another word for the eggplant, deriving from the French *auberge*, a kind of peach, possibly because the first cultivated eggplants were about the size of a peach. *Aubergine* is also used as an adjective meaning "black" or "dark purple." *See* EGGPLANT.

audible edibles. A humorous name for popcorn. According to his obituary in the *New York Times* (February 19, 2004), Samuel Rubin (1919–2004), known as "Sam the Popcorn Man," was largely responsible for the sale of popcorn in U.S. movie theaters. "Movies had prospered without popcorn until the Great Depression, when theater owners scrambled to make up for reduced ticket prices by turning to 'audible edibles,'" Douglas Martin wrote in Rubin's obituary. "The appetite of moviegoers was so great that from 1934 to 1940 the nation's annual popcorn harvest grew from 5 million to 100 million pounds."

avocado. When Montezuma served the *avocado*, or alligator pear, to Cortés and his conquistadores, the Aztecs explained that their *ahucatl* was so named from their word meaning "testicle," not only because the fruit resembled a testicle but because it supposedly excited sexual passion. The Aztecs even drew their guests pictures to illustrate their story, but to the Spaniards *ahucatl* sounded like *avocado*, their word for "advocate," and they named it so when they brought it back to Spain. In Europe the *avocado* became a great favorite, and France's Sun King called it *la bonne poire* (the good pear) because it seemed to get a rise out of his setting libido. Aphrodisiac or not, the fruit remains an important meat substitute in parts of the world today and a delicious dessert in others.

B

Baby Ruth. The popular candy bar was probably named after BABE RUTH in 1921, when Ruth was already a legendary star. Soon after, Ruth challenged the naming, trying unsuccessfully to patent his own *Babe Ruth Home Run Bar,* and the candymaker then claimed its *Baby Ruth* had been named after President Grover Cleveland's daughter Ruth, widely called Baby Ruth. Since Baby Ruth had died in 1904, 17 years before the candy bar was marketed, such a naming seems highly unlikely. The Baby Ruth candy bar probably was named for Babe Ruth, even though the candymaker doesn't support the story anymore. Ira Berkow's "A Babe Ruth Myth . . ." (*New York Times* 4/7/02) tells the story in greater detail.

back to the salt mines! Back to work, especially dreary, unrewarding work, "slave labor." This catchphrase may be several hundred years old. It originated in Russia, where people have been punished for centuries by banishment to Siberia and compulsory labor in the salt mines there. The phrase is, however, first recorded in an 1890s play about Russian exiles in Siberia.

bacon and rice aristocracy. A nickname for those who made great fortunes raising these commodities or selling them.

bad egg; good egg. Shakespeare used the word *egg* to contemptuously describe a young person in *Macbeth,* when the murderers of Macduff's son cry, "What you egg! Young fry of treachery!" But the expression *bad egg* for a disreputable, thoroughly rotten person doesn't seem to have been coined until the mid-18th century in America, no matter how obvious the analogy might seem.

"American criminal Thomas Egg" isn't in any way responsible for the expression; it derives from just the odor of a bad egg itself. *Good egg,* for a "nice guy," came along about 50 years later, probably originating as Oxford University slang.

bagel; bialy. "Bagels, BEGORRAH!" Macy's bakery once advertised on St. Patrick's Day in our word-rich land. *Bagel* derives from the Middle High German *bouc,* "bracelet," which became the Yiddish *beggel*—the *bagel,* of course, resembling a bracelet in shape. The roll topped with onion flakes called a bialy (plural bialys, not bialies) takes its name from Bialystok, Poland, where it was first made. Bialystok, played by Zero Mostel in *The Producers,* is one of the great comic characters in movie history.

baked alaska. Consisting of ice cream mounded on a cake base placed briefly in a hot oven to brown its blanket of meringue, baked alaska is among the most posh of desserts. It was created and named at New York's Delmonico's restaurant in 1876 in honor of the newly purchased Alaskan territory. An informant advises that a blow torch is now commonly used to make it. As my informant notes—nouvelle cuisine indeed!

baker's dozen. Bakers in ancient times were subject to severe penalties for shortweighting their customers; in ancient Egypt, for example, they were sometimes nailed by the ear to the doors of their shops when caught selling light loaves. Thus when the English Parliament passed a law in 1266 subjecting the Company of White Bakers and the Company of Brown Bakers to strict regulations regarding bread weight, the bakers made sure that they complied. Since it was difficult to make loaves of a uniform weight at the time, bakers customarily added a thirteenth loaf, the "in-bread" or "vantage loaf," to each shipment of 12 they sent to a shop keeper or retailer, thus guaranteeing that there would be no shortchanging or earnailing. Most authorities believe this led to the expression *baker's dozen* for 13.

bamboo. Linnaeus adopted the Maylay name *bambu* for these giant grasses, giving the name to the plant's genus, which consists of about 120 species and whose name has come to be spelled *bamboo*, probably in error. The tropical bamboos range from 15 to 100 feet in height. An interestingly named bamboo is the Chinese *Buddha's belly bamboo* (*Bambusa ventricosa*). *Bambis oldhamii*, *Oldham's bamboo*, is grown for the excellent flavor of its shoots. In the U.S. the native bamboo is called a *cane*, including the *sugar cane*, which often forms impenetrable *canebrakes* 15 to 25 feet high in the South.

banana. *Banana* derives from the Arabic word *banana*, meaning finger, and even today the individual fruits forming the familiar banana "hand" are called "fingers." The banana tree is really a giant herb with a rhizome instead of roots, and its "trunk" is made up of large leaves, not wood. The fruit was given the scientific name *Musa*, comprising 18 species, by Linnaeus in honor of Antonio Musa, personal physician to the first emperor of Rome. *Musa sapientum*, the most common banana tree species, takes its second name from the Latin word for "wise man," in reference to the Indian sages of old who reposed in its shade and ate of its fruit. Arabian slang and a score of other languages make the fruit a synonym for the male sexual organ, not surprisingly, and "I had a banana with Lady Diana" was British slang for sexual intercourse up until about 1930. "Where the banana grows man is sensual and

cruel," Emerson wrote in his *Society and Solitude*, and the Koran says that the forbidden fruit in Paradise was a banana, not an apple. Banana oil, incidentally, is a synthetic—bananas produce no commercial oil—and the banana, like the pear, is one of the few fruits that ripen better off the tree.

banana slug. The slug *Ariolimax columvianus*. William Least Heat Moon in *Blue Highways* (1982) wrote of an Oregon area: "I poked about the woods and turned up a piece of crawling yellow jelly nearly the length of my hand. It was a banana slug, so named because the mollusk looks like a wet, squirming banana."

banana oil. Nonsense, foolishness. An obituary of the syndicated advice columnist Ann Landers (Eppie Lederer, 1918–02) noted that she never made public expressions of annoyance "much stronger than 'oh banana oil!'"

bangers and mash. Visitors to Australia sometimes mistake this for an alcoholic drink, but it is simply Australian for a dish of sausage and mashed potatoes. The Australians and British call sausages *bangers* because they often split open with a slight bang while cooking.

barbecue. Here's an English word that comes from the language of the extinct Haitian Taino tribe. The tribe smoked meat on a framework of sticks called a *barbacoa*—at least the name sounded like that to Spanish pirates who visited Haiti in the mid-17th century. *Barbacoa* came to mean the cooking of the meat itself and passed into English as the American *barbecue.* The Tainos also gave us the word POTATO, which was first their *batata.*

bare as a milkpan when the cat's been round. Impoverished. "That farm's always 'bout as bare as a milkpan when the cat's been round."

Bartlett pear; Seckel pear. The yellow Bartlett grown commercially mostly in Oregon and Washington, where it is less susceptible to blight than in the East, represents 70 percent of the country's 713,000-ton crop and is certainly America's most commonly grown pear. It is a soft European-type fruit, in season from July to November, as opposed to earlier hard Asian varieties like the Seckel, which is named for the Philadelphia farmer who first grew it in America just after the Revolution. The Bartlett was not, in fact, developed by Enoch Bartlett (1779–1860), a merchant in Dorchester, Massachusetts, as is generally believed. Bartlett only promoted the fruit after Captain Thomas Brewer imported the trees from England and grew them on his Roxbury farm. The enterprising Yankee eventually purchased Brewer's farm and distributed the pears under his own name in the early 1800s. They had been long known in Europe as Williams or William Bon Chrétien pears. Bartletts, by any name, are one of the most delicious of the over 3,000 pear species, and pears have been one of man's favorite fruits from as early as 1000 B.C.

basil. Basil was once believed to have been used in making royal perfume, and so the aromatic herb takes its name from the Greek *basilikos,* royal. In ancient times it was thought to have great healing properties. Boccaccio's *Decameron* tells the story of Isabella, who put her murdered lover's head in a pot, planted basil on top, and watered it with her tears.

bay scallop. The aristocrat of scallops, especially the unsurpassed Peconic Bay scallop of Long Island, New York, across Long Island Sound from New England. Bay scallops are found from the estuaries of Long Island Sound up to the coast of Cape Cod, Nantucket, and Martha's Vineyard.

beach plum. A shrub (*Prunus maritime*) growing near the shore, its fruit used in making preserves. Also an old name for the bunchberry (*Cornus canadensis*), a low-growing plant with scarlet berries.

bean; string bean; green bean. Deriving from the Old English *bean,* and possibly akin to the Latin *faba* by a circuitous route, *bean* was long used for the seeds of many plants. "Common beans" (string beans, first recorded in 1759; Lima beans; wax beans; etc.) are native to the Americas. Napoleon wouldn't eat string beans, afraid that he would choke on the strings, but today's varieties are virtually stringless and thus are often called green beans. As early as 1830, one observer noted: "We do not call it a string bean, because the pod is entirely stringless." Yet *string bean* is still used for the vegetable and Americanisms like *string bean* for a tall, thin person remain in the language. *Bean pole,* another Americanism for a lanky person, takes its name from the tall poles that support climbing bean plants.

Beaneater; Boston baked beans. Since at least the late 19th century, *Beaneater* has been a humorous nickname for a Bostonian, Boston being called *Beantown. Boston baked beans* have been regarded as the best of baked beans for a half century longer and are still so thought today. They are made basically with navy beans flavored with molasses and slowly cooked with pork. Baked beans have been the traditional Saturday night supper in New England since early times, the left-over traditionally being part of Sunday breakfast.

beanfeast. No one is sure about beanfeast's derivation. The annual dinner that British employers gave their workers in the 1800s may be so named because beans were served at the feast or because a "bean goose," a goose "with a beak like a horse bean," was part of the fare. On the other hand, *bean* here may come from *bene,* "prayer, solicitation," because charitable collections were made at the feasts.

beanpole. Another Americanism for a tall, thin person, *beanpole* takes its name from the tall poles that support climbing bean plants.

beans and bullets. What the army travels on. The "beans" in the old U.S. saying means food in general.

beef Stroganoff; beef Wellington. Nineteenth-century Russian diplomat Count Paul Stroganoff has the

honor of having the well-known *beef Stroganoff* named after him. It is beef sauteed with onions and cooked in a sauce of consommé, sour cream, mushrooms, mustard, and other condiments. *Beef Wellington,* another popular dish, commemorates Arthur Wellesley, first duke of Wellington, whose name is part of a number of terms, including wellington boots. *Beef Wellington* combines a choice cut of beef, liver pâté, bacon, brandy, and various condiments, all baked in a golden crust of puffed pastry.

beefeater. The popular name of the warders of the Tower of London and the Yeoman of the Guard, all of whom dress in 15thcentury uniforms and are perennial tourist attractions. Their name, however, was originally a derogatory term for a well-fed servant, something of a glutton, and three centuries ago the French used it as a contemptuous word for an English soldier.

beer. *Beer* possibly derives from the Latin *biber,* for "drink." Roman soldiers most likely demanded *biber* in taverns wherever they went in Germany and the tavern owners assumed that this meant the ale in which they specialized. Gradually, the German word for ale became *biber* and then *Bier,* which came into English as *beer.*

beer and skittles. Mainly a British tavern game of ninepin in which a wooden ball or disk is used to knock down the pins, skittles takes its name from the Scandinavian *skutill,* "shuttle." This game, similar to shuffleboard, has been played since the early 17th century in taverns, where *beer and skittles* became an expression for a relaxed, laid-back lifestyle in which people want no more from life, and no less, than their beer and a game of skittles. Life sometimes gives more, of course, and frequently gives less.

beerbelly. A big stomach or potbelly that is attributed to drinking too much beer over the years. Called a *booze belly* in some regions.

beet; red as a beet. *Beet* comes to us from the Greek *beta,* for a similar plant. *Red as a beet* has probably been used as long as man has used beets. The French *betterave,* "beet," has served as slang for the penis, an analogy not unknown in history, despite the unlikely shape of the modern beet for such—Catullus wrote about a Roman matron who left her husband because the object of her desires "dangled like a limp beet."

bender. Though most benders, or drunken sprees, take place on land today, the word has nautical origins. Before it came ashore it was a sailor's word for a drinking bout, first recorded in the 19th century.

betel nut. The betel nut is a famous masticatory that people prize for the joy of a stimulating chew, even though it turns their teeth pitch-black. It comes from the areca or betel palm *(Areca catechu);* the tree's fruit, roughly the size of a hen's egg, contains the mottled gray seed or nut. The nuts are boiled, sliced, and dried in the sun until they turn black or dark brown, when they are ready to be wrapped up in betel leaves and chewed. Native to Malaya and southern India, betel nuts are so widely used in Asian nations that it is estimated that 1/10th of all the people on earth indulge in betel chewing. The introduction of modern chewing gum has cut into this figure slightly, but the betel chewers aren't easily discouraged, not by the copious flow of brick-red saliva caused by chewing the betel nuts, which dye the lips, mouth, and gums, nor by all those black teeth resulting from a betel nut habit. Betel is a true excitant and arouses a great craving in the addict. Legions of devotees—black-toothed, bloody-mouthed, and bad-breathed—can still be seen throughout Asia chomping away and squirting scarlet juice on the walls.

Bibb lettuce. An amateur gardener named John B. Bibb developed Bibb lettuce in his backyard garden in Frankfort, Kentucky, about 1850, and the variety has been an American favorite ever since. Bibb is the most famous and best of what are called butterhead lettuces, having a tight small head of dark green color and a wonderful flavor.

Because the variety is inclined to bolt in hot weather, a summer Bibb is now offered by nurserymen for the home garden. Several kinds of lettuce are named after their developers, including blackseeded Simpson, a loose-leaf variety. The vegetable can be traced back to ancient India and Central Asia, but takes its name from the Latin word *lac,* meaning silk, the Romans favoring lettuce for its milky juice and calling it *lactuce.* Bibb is not often found in the market, the most popular sellers in the United States being iceberg lettuce, a heading variety, and loose-leaf Boston lettuce.

big butter-and-egg man. Speakeasy owner Texas Guinan may have coined this expression for a wealthy big spender during the Roaring Twenties. According to the story, one of her patrons kept buying rounds for the house all evening and showering $50 bills on the chorus girls. Texas asked him to take a bow but he would only identify himself as being in the dairy business, so Texas put the spotlight on him, asking for "a hand for my big butter-and-egg man." In any case, George S. Kaufman used the phrase as the title of a play in 1925, giving it greater currency.

the Big Apple. A nickname for New York City since the 1960s, *the Big Apple* was first used in New Orleans. In about 1910 jazz musicians there used it as a loose translation of the

Spanish *manzana principal,* the main "apple orchard," the main city block downtown, the place where all the action is.

big cheese. A *big cheese,* for "a boss or important person," is an Americanism dating back to about 1890. But it derives from the British expression *the cheese,* meaning "the thing or the correct thing, the best." The British expression, in turn, is a corruption of the Persian or Urdu *chiz* (or *cheez*), "thing," that the British brought back from India in about 1840. A *big cheese* thus has nothing to do with cheese and should properly be "a big chiz."

big enchilada. A person who is the boss, the head man or woman, the big shot of any organization. The term is first recorded on one of the Watergate tapes in 1973, the speaker, John Ehrlichman, referring to Attorney General John Mitchell. In a letter from jail to author William Safire, Ehrlichman later claimed he had coined the expression, having "cooked my own enchiladas for years" as part of his "California upbringing." Possibly the term owes something to the phrase *the whole enchilada*—everything, the whole ball of wax—which had been around at least seven years longer, first recorded in 1966. Other foodstuffs associated with bossdom include *big banana, big cheese, big fish, big potato,* and *big vegetable,* among others. An *enchilada,* an American Spanish word, is a tortilla rolled and stuffed with cheese, meat, or beans and served with a hot chili sauce.

Bing cherry. *Bing cherries* are popular dark red, nearly black fruit of the Bigarreau or firm, crisp-fleshed group. The tree was developed in 1875 by a Chinese farmer named Bing in Oregon, where over a quarter of the United States's sweet cherry crop is grown. Other cherry varieties named after their developers include the Luelling, for the man who founded Oregon's cherry industry in 1847, the Lambert, and the Schmidt. Countless varieties honor famous people, such as the "Napoleon," the "Royal Ann," and the "Governor Wood," though none is named for George Washington. Surprisingly, sour cherries outnumber sweets two to one in the United States because they are easier to grow and are more in demand for cooking and canning. Cherries were probably first cultivated in China over 4,000 years ago, so Bing was carrying on a great ethnic tradition.

biltong. Animal lovers will not much like this South African word (from the Dutch *bil,* buttock, plus *tong,* tongue, meaning a strip of filet). In South Africa *biltong* is usually strips of air-dried and salted wild game meat. There is shark biltong, ostrich biltong, lion biltong, elephant biltong, and many other types. Elephants culled from the herds in Kruger National Park are often sold to butchers. The meat of "an elephant facing due east" when shot is said to be particularly tasty for some reason, or superstition. *See* JERKEY.

bird's nest soup. This most recherché of gourmet soups is definitely made from bird's nests—notably those of swallows of the genus *Collichia,* whose nests are glutinous half-cups composed of the spawn of fish and seaweed bound together by the birds' cementlike saliva. The swiftlings whose nests are used for the soup are mainly found on the island of Borneo, where literally millions live in great systems of limestone caves, their nests of solidified saliva stuck to the walls. The nests of the swifts are thought to be a gourmet aphrodisiac because they are the only nonhuman bird known to make love on the wing. After being collected, the nests are washed in hot water and rubbed with ground nut oil to help remove feathers and dirt. They must be soaked for two hours before they swell and become transparent for use in bird's nest soup. When the soup cooks, the nests fall to pieces, giving the soup its characteristic viscid texture.

biscuit. Biscuits were cooked a second time to keep them from quickly spoiling at sea. Thus their name derives from the French *biscuit,* "cooked twice."

Bismarck herring. Often served as a cold hors d'oeuvre, this dish is salted filet of herring, pickled in vinegar, white wine, and spices.

bistro. When the Russians invaded Paris after Napoleon I's fall in 1815, restaurant owners or their shills would lure them into their places by shouting the Russian word *bystro,* meaning "quick," assuring them that they could eat quickly here at a good price. They used the word so often that it became altered to *bistro,* the common French word for any small unpretentious restaurant where cheap meals could be had, and from there bistro soon entered into English. But bistro could come from the French *bistoille,* cup of coffee. Or the word may derive from the French *bistouille,* raw spirits, for the cheap liquor served in such establishments. No one is sure.

black-eyed peas. So named for their black hilum, black-eyed peas *(Vigna sinensis)* are simply a variety of cowpeas that originated in India thousands of years ago (though the name "cowpea" originated in colonial America). George Washington grew these peas, which are actually botanically closer to the bean than the pea family. They are often cooked southern style: stewed with a bit of ham or pork fat. Black-eyed peas go by many names in the South, including "crowders," "black bean," "black-eyed bean," "black-eyed susan," "bung belly," "China bean," "cow bean," "cream pea" and even "chain-gang pea" because they are said to be fed to prisoners on chain gangs. *See* PEA.

bless the meat and damn the skin. Part of an old American grace said before a meal: "Bless the meat an' damn the skin, / Throw back your 'eads an' all pitch in."

blintz. Another delicious ethnic food that has become popular nationwide, thanks largely to its appearance in the frozen food sections of supermarkets. Ultimately *blintz* comes from the Ukranian *blints,* "pancake," which became the Yiddish *blintzeh* and was then shortened to *blintz.* A blintz in Jewish cookery is a thin pancake folded or rolled around a filling of cheese, potatoes, fruit, etc., fried or baked, and often served with sour cream. The word is also spelled *blintze.*

Bloody Mary. It is said, without much proof being offered, that this cocktail made from vodka and tomato juice takes its name from Mary I or Mary Tudor (1516–58), queen of England, who was nicknamed Bloody Mary. Not because she drank the concoctions (for one thing tomatoes were unknown in England at the time), but because she had some 300 of her subjects put to death during her reign, including a former queen and the archbishop of Canterbury. Another story claims that the potent drink was invented at the famous Harry's Bar in Paris in 1920 and named by an anonymous American expatriate who proposed that it be called the Bloody Mary because it reminded him of the Bucket of Blood Club in Chicago and he had a girl named Mary. The drink has since become famous as a hangover "remedy," the foremost example of the hair-of-the-dog-that-bit-you school. According to an article in *USA Today* on December 10, 1985, "The Bloody Mary made its debut in an ad that appeared in late December 1955. In it [New York entertainer] George Jessel declared that he invented the drink at 5 one morning." Bloody Mary is also the name of a character in James Michener's *Tales of the South Pacific* (1946).

bodock; Osage orange. *Bodock* is another name for the Osage orange tree *(Maclura pomifera)*. It is so called because the Indians used its wood for making bows and the French thus called it the *bois d'arc* ("bowwood") tree, which became corrupted in English to *bodock*. It is called the *Osage orange* because it grew in Osage Indian country and has large, rough-skinned greenish fruits somewhat suggestive of an orange, but inedible. The spiny-branched tree is often used for hedges and called the Osage thorn. It is first recorded, in 1804, by the Lewis and Clark expedition, as the Osage Apple.

boloney. Al Smith, governor of New York and unsuccessful presidential candidate in 1928, helped popularize this expression with his remark "No matter how you slice it, it's still baloney." But *boloney* for "bunk" dates back to at least the early 20th century, bologna sausage having been pronounced *boloney* as early as the 1870s, when there was a popular song "I Ate the Boloney." There are those who say that *boloney* for "bunk" has nothing to do with bologna sausage, however, tracing it to a corruption of the Spanish *pelone*, "testicles," and claiming that this meant "nonsense" or "bunk" just as "balls," "all balls," and "nerts" did. The word is also spelled *baloney*.

bon-bon. *Bon- bon* means "good, good" in French and the name was probably given to candies by children, "originating in the nursery," according to the *O.E.D.* The term is first recorded in Thomas Moore's satirical poem "The Fudge Family in Paris" (1818): "The land of Cocaigne . . . / Where for hail they have bon-bons, and claret for rain."

bonne-bouche. An English term since the 18th century, *bonne-bouche* means "a dainty or tasty mouthful or morsel." It comes from the French *bonne-bouche* (*bonne*, "good," plus *bouche*, "mouth"), which means "a pleasing taste in the mouth" in that language. French for a dainty morsel would be *morceau qui fait ou donne bonne bouche*.

bonnet squash. This common vegetable sponge *(Luffa cylindrica)* was so named in the American South because women made bonnets out of its fibrous matter. Wrote Joel Chandler Harris in *On the Plantation* (1892): "The girls made their hats of rye and wheat straw, and some very pretty bonnets were made of the fibrous substance that grew in the vegetable patch known as the bonnet squash." These inedible squashes are also called "dishcloth gourds" and "loofah." They are widely sold as sponges.

booze. Mr. E. G. or E. S. Booze of either Philadelphia or Kentucky, circa 1840, was a distiller who sold his *booze* under his own name, the bottles often made in the shape of log cabins. But *booze* probably has its roots in the Middle English verb *bousen*, "to drink deeply," which comes from an earlier German word. However, the English use *booze* only for beer and ale and there is no doubt that the labels on our Mr. Booze's bottles influenced the American use of the word for hard liquor and strengthened its general use. Today booze most often signifies cheap, even rotgut whiskey.

bosom bread. A historical term for the large flat loaves of bread that black hands working the Mississippi steamboats in the 19th century often carried inside their shirt fronts for snacks throughout the day. They needed such fuel, as these longshoremen expended more energy than almost any other workers at the time.

Boston baked beans. Famous since at least the mid-19th century as the best of baked beans, made with navy beans flavored with molasses and slowly cooked with pork. Baked beans have been the traditional Saturday night supper in New England since early times, though recipes for them vary greatly. Left over beans were traditionally Sunday breakfast fare.

botulism. Why, you ask, does the Latin word for sausage, *botulus,* give us the English word *botulism,* first recorded in 1878, for "a form of food poisoning"? The answer is that the earliest cases of such food poisoning through improperly stored food involved canned sausages.

bouillabaisse. A French invention made of fish and shellfish, *bouillabaisse* derives from Provençal words meaning "boil it, then lower the heat." It has a worldwide reputation. In Greece it is called *psaro,* in Italy it is *zuppa di pesce,* and in Belgium it's *Ghentsche waterzoaie.* In his *Gastronomy of France* chef Raymond Oliver tells the legend of the spurned lover who invented *rouille,* the hot pimento sauce that makes *bouillabaisse* so passionate a potage. This poor sailor sat on the Martigues quay, sadly watching his perfidious beloved sail off with a rich Greek shipowner (they've always been around) when she added humiliation to heartbreak by tossing him the liver of a *racasse,* or scorpion fish, that the yacht's cook had been cleaning on deck. "There, that's for you!" she cried scornfully. But the sailor treasured even the scraps from her hands, and crushing the liver with garlic and oil, he cooked it with pimento and—marvelous to relate—from the moment he first tasted it he found *all* women lovely. "As *rouille* increases *bouillabaisse's* erotic proportion a hundredfold," Oliver concludes, "the perfidious girl was forgotten on the spot. Once more, a fairy tale with a happy ending."

bourbon. *Bourbon whiskey* takes its name from Bourbon County, Kentucky, named for France's Bourbon kings, and home of the first still that produced it. The word *Bourbon* for a political reactionary also derives from France's Bourbon kings, a dynasty that reigned for over 200 years beginning in 1589, and of whom it was said that they "forgot nothing and learned nothing." The *Dictionary of Americanisms* gives its first use for a political diehard as 1876.

Bourbon Street. Another storied American street, this one named for the French Bourbon kings (see bourbon above). In *Love and Money* (1954), Erskine Caldwell called the noted New Orleans street "that Southern gentleman's skid row."

boysenberry. Americans have always been pie makers without peer, thanks to sugar resources close by, an abundance of native fruit, and a willingness to experiment. The blackberry, long regarded as a nuisance and called a bramble or brambleberry in England, is a case in point. Many varieties of blackberries have been developed here, long before anyone paid attention to the family *Rubus* in Europe. Among them is the boysenberry, a prolific, trailing variety that is a cross between the BLACKBERRY, RASPBERRY, and LOGANBERRY, another eponymous berry. The boysenberry, a dark wine-red fruit that tastes something like a raspberry, was developed by California botanist Rudolf Boysen in the early 1900s. Single plants commonly produce two quarts of the large 3/4-inch round, 11/2-inch-long fruit.

brandy. *Brandy* is a shortening of *brandywine,* which comes from the Dutch *brandewijn. Brandewijn,* in turn, derives from the Dutch *branden,* "burn" and *wijn,* "wine," translating as "burned (or distilled) wine." The word is first recorded in the early 17th century.

bread. As a synonym for money, *bread* is an underworld term, first recorded in 1935 but not widely used until the late 1950s. Several English proverbs equating *bread* with one's livelihood, such as *taking the bread out of someone's mouth,* could have

suggested the coinage, or, more likely, it may have been suggested by the common term *dough* for money.

bread crumbs; fork in the beam. Naval discipline was much harder to take a century or so ago. For instance, when a British senior officer used the expression *Bread crumbs!* at that time, it was a signal that junior midshipmen in their mess were not allowed to hear what was going to be said next and actually had to stuff their ears with bread until the senior officers finished speaking. Similarly, when a senior officer placed a fork in the beam (above his head), it meant that he wanted privacy, and all junior midshipmen had to leave the mess. *See* FORK.

bread (or toast) never falls but on its buttered side. This bemoaning of bad luck may be a much older proverb, but the idea is immortalized in a 1884 poem by English author James Payn (1830–98), who wrote over 100 novels as well as a volume of poems and several nonfiction works:

> I had never had a piece of toast
> Particularly long and wide,
> But fell upon the sanded floor,
> and always on the buttered side.

bread and circuses. *Bread and circuses* is a translation of a line by the Roman poet Juvenal that refers to the practice in ancient Rome of government feeding the people and providing them with entertainment to prevent rebellion. The term means the same today.

breadfruit. Breadfruit *(Artocarpus incisa),* which grows wild on trees on South Pacific islands, was so named because English seamen who sampled the fruit in the 17th century believed its soft white pulp resembled fresh baked bread—although it tastes something like sweet potato.

breadline. In *The Dictionary of Americanisms, breadline* is said to have been first recorded in 1900, but no specific account of its origin offered. However, in his fascinating book *Here at the New Yorker,* Brendan Gill attributes the expression to the Fleischmann family from whose yeast fortune rose the *New Yorker* magazine. The family ran the Vienna Model Bakery in New York City during the late 1870s: "In order to call attention to the freshness of Fleischmann's bread and also, it appears, because of an innate generosity, Lewis [Fleischmann] made a practice of giving away at 11 every evening what ever amount of bread had not been sold during the day. The poor lined up to receive it at the bakery door; hence our word 'breadline.' " The term had its widest use during the Great Depression 50 years later.

breadwinner; bread. *Breadwinner* is one of the few words still retaining the meaning of the Anglo-Saxon word *winnan,* "to toil," that gives us the word "win"—a breadwinner being one who toils to obtain bread. As slang for money, *bread* dates back to about 1935 and may derive from the Cockney rhyming slang "bread and honey," for money.

break the ice. Ice skaters might test the ice in a rink, but would never break it, and so have nothing to do with this expression meaning to be the first to try something, or to break a silence or uneasiness when people meet, etc. The allusion is probably either to ice being sold for the first time in America, in the 1830s, when *to break the ice* came to mean to introduce

brie. The delicious cheese is named for Brie, an agricultural district in France noted for its cheese and other dairy products.

bring home the bacon. An English custom initiated in 1111 and lasting until late in the 18th century provided that any married couple who swore that they hadn't quarreled for over a year, or had not at any time wished themselves "single again"—and could prove this to the satisfaction of a mock jury sometimes composed of six bachelors and six maidens—was entitled to the Dunmow Flitch, a side of bacon awarded at the church of Dunmow in Essex County. The expression to *bring home the bacon,* "to win the prize," isn't recorded until 1925, but bacon was used as a word for "prize" centuries before, and most scholars believe that the Dunmow Flitch is responsible for the usage. This custom, along with the popular American one of awarding the pig to the winner of "greased-pig" events at county fairs, gives us the phrase, which now means to support a family by working.

broccoli. Roman farmers, who must have been more poetic than their contemporary counterparts, are said to have called *broccoli* "the five green fingers of Jupiter." The word has a more prosaic derivation, however, coming from the Latin *bracchium,* "a strong arm or branch," in reference to its shape. According to Pliny the Elder, Drusus, the eldest son of Emperor Tiberius ate so much broccoli that his urine turned bright green! *See* I SAY IT'S SPINACH AND I SAY THE HELL WITH IT.

brown-eyed peas. These are black-eyed peas with a brown rather than black spot where they were attached to the pod. They also go by the name "brown-eyed crowder peas." Regardless, they always taste just like black-eyed peas. *See* BLACK-EYED PEAS.

brunch. *Brunch* is a dictionary-accepted word for a meal. Brunch came into the language back in 1895, when it was introduced in *Hunter's Weekly,* a British publication, to describe a combined breakfast and luncheon. It had probably been a collegiate coinage a little earlier. *Lupper,* a mid afternoon meal eaten instead of lunch and supper, is a new portmanteau word "struggling to be born," according to William Sherk in *500 Years of New Words* (1983). *Dunch* and *blupper* are two possible substitutes for *lupper,* suggested by readers of Marian Burros's "De Gustibus" column in the *New York Times.*

Brunswick stew. A stew of squirrel meat, lima beans, and green corn seasoned with salt and pepper and said to have been invented by a cook in Brunswick County, Virginia, over 100 years ago.

brussels sprout. Unknown in America until about 1800, this relatively "new" vegetable is named for the capital of Belgium, where it was developed or improved upon early in the 16th century.

bumper crop. *Bumper,* in the sense of "something large," is only heard today in the expression *a bumper crop,* one that is extraordinarily abundant, as in "We had a bumper crop of tomatoes."

Burbank; Burbank plum; Burbank potato. There has been muted controversy over whether the plant breeder Luther Burbank (1849–1926) was a "plant wizard" or something of a failure. Burbank was born in Lancaster, Massachusetts, and there developed the Burbank potato, his most

important achievement, while just a boy experimenting with seeds in his mother's garden. At 26 he moved to Santa Rosa, California, using the $150 he made from the sale of his potato to pay for the journey. It was in Santa Rosa, his "chosen spot of the earth," that he bred almost all the varieties of fruit, vegetables, and ornamentals for which he became famous. These included at least 66 new fruits, 12 new bush fruits, seven tree nuts, and nine vegetables, of which a number, notably the Burbank plum, bear his name. He once grew half a million strawberry plants to obtain one prize plant. However, according to Dr. W. L. Howard (University of California Agricultural Experiment Station Bulletin, 1945), only a few of the several hundred varieties developed by Burbank have stood the test of time. The patient Burbank was not the first American plant breeder—Thomas Jefferson, George Washington Carver, and Charles Hovey, originator of the Hovey strawberry, came long before him. Burbank was strongly influenced by Darwin's *The Variation of Animals and Plants Under Domestication.* His credo can be summed up in his statement "I shall be contented if, because of me, there shall be better fruits and fairer flowers." Burbank did have a sense of humor, unlike some of his critics. The renowned horticulturist was working in his experimental garden one day when approached by an obnoxious neighbor: "Well, what on earth are you working on now?" the man asked. "I'm trying to cross an eggplant and milkweed," Burbank replied. "What in heaven do you expect to get from that?" asked the neighbor. "Custard pie," said Burbank calmly. The city of Burbank, California was named for the famous plant breeder.

burgundy. Burgundy wines are usually red wines made from grapes from the French province of Burgundy, especially the area between Dijon and Chalons. The province, in turn, takes its name from the Medieval Latin *Burgundia,* land of the Burgunds (a German tribe). When one thinks of burgundy, one often remembers James Thurber's famous put-down in a caption to a *New Yorker* cartoon depicting a winesnob saying to another: "It's a naive domestic Burgundy without any breeding, but I think you'll be amused by its presumption."

burr artichoke. A globe or French artichoke, as opposed to a Jerusalem artichoke. The globe artichoke is used for making stuffed artichokes.

butterfingers. Although the word *butterfingers*—used for someone who drops things or can't hold on to anything, as if his fingers were coated with slippery butter—has been traced back to early-17th-century England, its popularity in America stems from its use as a baseball term for a fielder who drops the ball. The baseball usage is first recorded in 1888 and *butterfingers* was being generally and widely used shortly thereafter.

butterfly pea. A woody perennial vine of the pea family, the butterfly pea *(Clitoria mariana)* has pale blue flowers that appear as if upside down, the standard (the upper, broad and usually erect petal of a pea flower) much larger than the rest of the flowers. It takes its popular name from its imagined resemblance to a butterfly. One gardening guide says "the origin of [the genus name] *clitoria* is unprintable"; fortunately, it is not too difficult to figure out. *See* AVOCADO; PEA.

butter up. In the sense of bestowing fulsome flattery upon someone this phrase dates all the way back to Congreve's *Way of the World* (1700): "The squire that's buttered still is sure to be undone." It is probably a translation of the French *cirer,* which means the same.

butter wouldn't melt in her mouth. Men have been saying this about demure women since the early 16th century; in fact, Heywood listed it as a proverb in 1536: the lady so prim and proper, so cold, that is, that even a piece of soft butter wouldn't melt in her mouth. In *Pendennis* Thackeray used the expression with reference to a girl who "smiles and languishes," but today it isn't usually employed in the sense of suspiciously amiable. In fact, the phrase once had a longer form: "She looks like butter wouldn't melt in her mouth, but cheese won't choke her," i.e., she's really not fastidious at all, but in fact rather earthy.

by-two coffee shop. Any shop in the south of India where two customers can share a cup of coffee between them, one-half a cup each. Such economical shops are the Starbucks of the poor and/or struggling.

C

cabbage. Ask for a head of cabbage and you are repeating yourself, for *cabbage* means "head," the name of the vegetable deriving from the Old French *caboce,* "swollen head." *Caboce* itself comes from the Old French *boce,* "a swelling," the *ca* in the word very likely suggested by the Latin *caput,* meaning "head." Cabbage, probably the most ancient of vegetables, has been cultivated for more than 4,000 years. In Greek mythology it is said to have sprung from sweat on the head of Jupiter. The Greeks also believed that eating it cured baldness.

cabbage head. Describing a fool as a *cabbage head* dates back to the late 17th century and is best explained by the old music-hall lyrics: "I ought to call him a cabbage head, / He is so very green . . ."

cabbages and kings. This expression meaning "odds and ends," "anything and everything," was used by O. Henry as the title for his first book of stories. It comes from Lewis Carroll's *Through the Looking Glass:*

> "The time has come," the Walrus said,
> "To talk of many things:
> Of shoes and ships—and sealing wax—
> Of cabbages—and kings—
> And why the sea is boiling hot—
> And whether pigs have wings."

cackleberry. A humorous American designation for eggs, dating back a century or so. It is said to have originated in early logging camps.

Caesar salad. This popular salad was not named after Julius Caesar nor any of his family. It seems to have been invented in the late 1920s by Caesar Gardini, a restaurant owner in Tijuana, Mexico, but there are several contenders for the honor.

Anchovies weren't included in the original Caesar recipe; the ingredients were Romaine lettuce, eggs, Romano cheese, croutons, olive oil, lemon juice, and condiments.

Caesar's mushroom. *Amanita caesaria* or Caesar's mushroom, honoring Julius Caesar, happens to be one species of the deadly *Amanita* genus that is edible, but more than a few "experts" have been poisoned thinking that they had distinguished this delicacy from its deadly relatives. Every summer brings scores of deaths from mushroom poisoning. Hippocrates referred to cases of mushroom poisoning in his day, and Horace warned the ancients to beware of all fungi, no matter how appetizing the appearance. One of the first recorded cases of mushroom poisoning occurred in the family of the Greek poet Euripides, who lost his wife, two sons and a daughter when they partook of a deadly *Amanita* species. Pope Clement VII, the Emperor Jovian, Emperor Charles VI, Czar Alexander I, the wife of Czar Alexis, and the Emperor Claudius (his niece and wife Agrippina poisoned his *boleti*) are among historical figures who lost their lives in the same way. Many species of *Amanita* are lethal even when eaten in minuscule amounts, and *Amanita verna,* the destroying angel, is easily confused with *Amanita caesaria* and the several other edible species. *See* MUSHROOM.

cafeteria. A relatively young Americanism, *cafeteria* was probably introduced in 1893 at the Chicago World's Fair. It derives, however, from the Spanish *cafetería,* meaning the same.

café society. Said to be coined one night in 1919 by newspaper society columnist Cholly Knickerbocker (Maury Paul) when he saw a number of prominent socialites dining out at the Ritz-Carlton in midtown Manhattan. Up to that time, supposedly, most of this breed dined at home. Paramount Pictures later paid Lucius Beebe, another city newspaper columnist, $50,000 for using the term *café society* as the title of a movie starring Madeleine Carroll—thinking he had invented the expression. But it is fairly certain that Champagne Cholly (as Paul was also known) deserves the honor. He is also said to have invented glamour girl, an old standby, but is mostly responsible for such thankfully extinct cutesy coinages as sweetie sweets (nice people) and doughy dowagers (rich people).

cakebell. A glass or plastic container, often kept on a diner's counter, where pies and cakes are displayed and kept fresh. When a portion of one is sold, the pie or cake is put back under the cakebell. In his novel *The Road,* Cormac McCarthy tells of a cakebell with a severed human head in it.

cakes and ale. Long before it became the title of Somerset Maugham's novel, *Cakes and Ale* meant "fun or pleasant activity," as in "life isn't all cakes and ale." Shakespeare may have in-vented the expression, for he first recorded it in *Twelfth Night* (1600): "Dost thou think, because thou art virtuous, there shall be no more cakes and ale?"

California breakfast. A derogatory expression that, according to a January 1962 *Western Folklore* article, means "a cigarette and an orange."

calzone. A favorite Italian food, consisting of a crisp Italian pastry made from pizza dough and filled with mozzarella and ricotta cheese, among other ingredients. So named from the Italian *calzone* for "trousers" because of its resemblance in shape to one leg of a pair of pants.

candy. We know that candy of various kinds has been around for at least 4,000 years and that there are at least 2,000 varieties of it available today. It was probably the Greeks who brought the word *candy* into the language. It seems that a favorite of the troops of Alexander the Great was a Persian delicacy called *kand*— a sweet reed garnished with honey, spices, and coloring. The word candy itself either came to us from this *kand* that Alexander's men brought home to Greece, or from the old Arab word for sugar, *quand*.

canned milk. Condensed milk in a can. When canned milk came out, one cowpuncher had written in praise of it:

> No tits to pull
> No hay to pitch,
> Just punch a hole
> In the son of a bitch.

can of corn. A high, easy-to-catch flyball or pop-up. There are numerous explanations for this baseball expression, first recorded in the early 1920s. Paul Dickson's excellent *The Dickson Baseball Dictionary* (1989) discusses several, including the theory that the phrase comes "from the old time grocery store where the grocer used a pole or a mechanical grabber to tip an item, such as a can of corn, off a high shelf and let it tumble into his hands or his apron, which was held out in front like a fire net." The term is also used outside of baseball today, meaning any easy accomplishment.

cannoli. To be good, this Italian pastry has to be crispy when filled with its mixture of ricotta cheese, cream, candied fruits, and other ingredients. It shouldn't be filled hours before, which makes its shell soggy. The cannoli has become a popular "international food" today. The pastry is named from the Italian *cannolo* for "tube," being tubular in shape. However, *cannoli* is never used in the singular form, although one such pastry should technically be a *cannolo*.

cantaloupe. The melon called a cantaloupe in the United States is not a cantaloupe. The cantaloupe, a variety of muskmelon, is named for Cantalupo, the Pope's country seat near Rome, where the melon was first bred in Italy from an Armenian variety. True cantaloupes are only grown in Europe. The "cantaloupe" grown in the United States is really the netted or nutmeg muskmelon, which originated in Persia (Iran). Muskmelons were introduced to America by Columbus, who brought seeds to Hispaniola on his second voyage; the many delicious varieties of muskmelon include the honeydew, Persian, casaba, and banana melons.

can't cut the mustard; can't cut (hack) it. Whatever the origins of *can't cut the mustard*, and they are about as clear as mustard, the expression *too old to cut the mustard* is always applied to men today and conveys the idea of sexual inability. *Can't cut the mustard*, however, means not to be able to handle any job for any reason, not just because of old age. Preceding the derivation of *too old to cut the mustard* by about a half a century, it derives from the expression *to be the mustard.* "Mustard" was slang for the "genuine article" or "main attraction" at the time. Perhaps someone cutting up to show that he was the *mustard,* or the greatest, was said *to cut the mustard* and the phrase later came to mean to be able to fill the

bill or do the important or main job. In any case, O. Henry first used the words in this sense in his story "Heart of the West" (1907) when he wrote: "I looked around and found a proposition that exactly cut the mustard." Today *can't cut the mustard* is usually *can't cut it or can't hack it.* A recent variant on *too old to cut the mustard is if you can't cut the mustard, you can lick the jar.*

Cape Cod turkey. New Englanders have called baked codfish Cape Cod turkey for many years, at least since the mid-19th century, just as melted cheese has been called WELSH RABBIT the world over.

cappuccino. This Italian espresso coffee mixed with steamed milk or cream is so called because its color resembles the color of the habits worn by the CAPUCHIN monks.

carrot. From the Latin *carota* for the vegetable, which derives from the Greek *karoton.* When carrots were first brought to England, women liked to use the plant's fern-like leaves as hair decorations, but didn't much care for them as food. The ancient Greeks extolled them as "love medicine" and called them *philtron.*

casaba. A variety of winter melon with a wrinkled skin and sweet, juicy green flesh. It is named after Kassaba (now Turgutlo), Turkey, where it was first grown about 1885. Also called "casaba melon" and "cassaba."

Catawba grapes; Concord. A light reddish variety of grape grown in the eastern United States, the Catawba was developed by John Adlum in his vineyard near Georgetown in 1829, its dominant parent being the northern fox grape. It was named three years later for the Catawba Indians of the Carolinas, or for the Catawba River, which takes its name from the Indian tribe. The Catawba, long a traditional favorite, contains some vinifera blood and is one of the best grapes for white domestic wines. By 1860, nine-tenths of all grapes grown east of the Rockies were Catawbas, but they were thereafter replaced by the Concord, perfected in 1850, as the leading American variety.

catch a crab. When an oarsman *catches a crab* he of course doesn't literally catch one on his oar. The expression, dating back to the 19th century, means that the oarsman has slowed down the speed of the boat either by missing the water on a stroke, or, more commonly, by making a poor, awkward stroke that doesn't completely clear the water when completed.

cauliflower. Cultivated for some 2,000 years, cauliflower takes its name from the Latin *caulis,* "cabbage," and *floris,* "flower." Its delicate flavor led Mark Twain to call it "cabbage with a college education." It is a relative youngster, however, when compared with cabbage, which has been grown for more than 4,000 years. *See* CABBAGE.

cauliflower ear. The white, gnarled scar tissue that forms on an ear repeatedly injured by boxing gloves gives that deformed ear the look of a head of cauliflower. The term has been around for a century or so and is even used by doctors to describe the condition.

caviar. *Caviar* derives from the Persian *khavyar,* salted sturgeon eggs. The Russians call the fish eggs *ikra,* not caviar, and it is from a select sturgeon species called the beluga that the highly regarded Beluga caviar comes. Actually, the most prized caviar of all is that made from selected golden sterlet's eggs of the *Acipenser ruthenus* species, produced by sterlets "with a particularly happy frame of mind." While dispelling myths about caviar, we should mention that *malossol* isn't a quality name like Beluga; it is just less salty caviar, and you can buy Beluga malossol, Sevruga malossol, et cetera.

caviar to the general. "I heard thee speak me a speech once," Hamlet says to the players at Elsinore, "but it was never acted . . . ; for the play, I remember, pleased not the million, 'twas caviar to the general." When Shakespeare says "general" here, he means the general public, the generality, the masses as they were later called, not the general of an army. The play he refers to (which was actually pretty bad, judging by the fragments presented) is, like caviar, for the tastes of only the most discriminating people; others would find it repugnant because they haven't acquired fine tastes. The rather snobbish remark is still commonplace in describing something for which one has to acquire a taste.

of breakfast tables. Ceres' Greek counterpart was Demeter, the goddess of fruit, crops, and vegetables.

celery. Celery is the *selinon* mentioned by Homer in the *Odyssey,* but the word comes to us directly from the French *céléri,* a derivation from the Greek word for the vegetable. Celery has been cultivated for centuries and its wild form, smallage, has been gathered in its native Mediterranean home for thousands of years. The Greeks held bitter smallage in high esteem and awarded stalks of it to winners of athletic contests.

cereal. Gardeners have prayed to many garden deities through the ages. After a drought ruined crops in 496 B.C., Roman priests insisted that a new goddess named Ceres be wor-shipped and prayed to for rain. When the drought ended, Ceres became protector of the crops and the first grains harvested each year were sacrificed to her and called *cerealis,* meaning "of Ceres." From *cerealis* came the English word *cereal,* which honors the goddess every   morning   on   millions

champagne. As defined by French law only sparkling wine produced from grapes grown in the French province of Champagne can, strictly speaking, be called champagne. It must be fermented in the bottle and varies from *brut,* the driest, to sweeter *doux* champagnes. Champagne has been called "the wine of love," "the wine of the gods," "the devil's wine," "the laugh of a pretty girl," "the only wine that leaves a woman beautiful after drinking it," and "the barometer of happiness." It is of course produced all over the world today and is still "the wine of wines," the most celebrated of all festive drinks. DOM PÉRIGNON is said to have cried out when he first tasted his historic version of it, "Come quickly, I am tasting stars!"

charlotte russe; apple charlotte. Marie-Antoine Carême, the greatest chef of his day, created a lavish pastry that he called the apple charlotte, after England's Princess Charlotte,   George   IV's   only daughter. The master chef apparently could not forget Charlotte, for while serving Czar Alexander in Russia, he created a jellied custard set in a crown of ladyfingers that he named the charlotte russe in her honor. Carême's creations were so valued that it is said that they were stolen from the table at the court of George IV—not to be relished at home, but to be sold in the market at high prices.

cheddar. Originally a cheese made in the village of Cheddar in England's Somerset County, *cheddar* today refers to "a wide variety of hard, crumbly cheeses ranging in flavor from mild to sharp and in color from yellow to orange." The word is first recorded in 1666, but the cheese probably was made long before then.

cheese. Clift on Fadiman wrote that cheese is "milk's leap to immortality." The word *cheese* itself comes from the Latin *caseus* for the food, whose origin dates back several thousand years before Christ. One legend claims that cheese was discovered by a traveling merchant named Kanana. When he started on one long trip, Kanana put his supply of milk in a pouch made of a sheep's stomach. The heat and shaking of the pouch on the journey, plus the rennet in the lining of the stomach, caused the curds in the milk to separate from the whey, and when he sat down to eat his lunch,

Kanana found delicious cheese. In any case, there are thousands of cheeses produced today. Most are named for the regions where they were born. Some important examples are Roquefort and Camembert, from France; Cheddar and Cheshire, from England; Edam from Holland; Muenster from Germany; Swiss from Switzerland; and Limburger from Limburg, Belgium. It would be impossible to list them all. In fact, France alone has enough varieties to fill a volume. French President Charles de Gaulle once remarked, "How can you govern a nation which has 246 kinds of cheese?"

cheesecake; beefcake. The old story is that in 1912 *New York Journal* photographer James Kane was developing a picture of an actress that included "more of herself than either he or she expected." As he looked at it, he searched for the greatest superlative he knew of to express his delight and exclaimed, "That's real cheesecake!" The word soon became synonymous with photographs of delectable models. In the 1970s, *beefcake* became the male equivalent.

cheese it, the cops! If you've ever wondered why *cheese* it means "stop it," or "watch it," Partridge has an answer for you. He suggests that the term, first recorded in England in 1812, is a mispronunciation of "cease it."

cherry. *Cherries* in English first meant *one cherry*, the word deriving from the French *cerise* (which came from the Latin *cerasus*) for the fruit. *Cerise* became *cherries*, but the *s* in *cherries* was dropped, because it made the singular word sound like a plural, and the result was *cherrie* or *cherry*. Much used as a simile in love poetry, from the Chinese poet Po Chu-i's "mouth like a red cherry," to Robert Herrick's "cherry ripe," the cherry surprisingly doesn't have much of a reputation as a love food. At least there are not many erotic recipes available using it, save for standards like cherry pie and Cherries Jubilee. The word, of course, has served as both a synonym for a young girl and a young woman's or young man's virginity.

The Cornelian cherry (*Cornus mas*) has exceedingly hard wood that is said to have been used for the Trojan horse, and its bark yields the red dye used for the traditional Turkish fez. Berries from a dwarf form of it were believed by the Scottish High-landers to create appetite, and they thus named the plant "Lus-a-chracis," Gaelic for "plant of gluttony."

cherry-picking. Discounters are often accused of "cherry-picking"— selling a great volume of a small selection of high turnover merchandise, or as *Fortune Magazine* once put it, a policy that concentrates only on fast-money, high-profit goods that are constantly in demand by an overwhelming majority of customers. "We're only giving the public what it wants," the discounters reply. The practice is sometimes called "creaming."

chew the fat (rag). One guess is that this expression was originally a nautical one: Sailors working their jaws on the tough salt pork rationed out when supplies ran low constantly grumbled about their poor fare while literally chewing the fat. *Chewing the rag* also had a grouchy connotation when first recorded in print at about the same time, in 1885. There are a few stories relating these words to actual rag chewing (men chewing pieces of rags when out of tobacco and grousing about it, etc.), but more than likely the expression has its roots in the English verb *to rag*, "to scold," its origin unknown. Both phrases are probably much older than their first appearance in print, and both are used more often today to mean a talkfest between friends than the act of complaining.

chicken. A game teenagers have played since at least the late 1940s in which two drivers (often with passengers) drive their cars directly at each other at high speed, the loser, or chicken, the one who first swerves out of the way. It can also be played by driving at telephone poles, etc., to see how narrowly a driver can avoid hitting them, and by racing another car toward a cliff, as famously depicted in the film *Rebel Without a Cause,* starring James Dean. The game takes its name from *to chicken out,* to back away in fear, CHICKEN-HEARTED or *chicken* as a slang synonym for a coward. The expression has often been used figuratively, as in the words of military expert Stephen Philip Cohen (12/23/01): "The Indians are playing chicken. They're counting on the United States to jerk the steering wheel so the Pakistanis do swerve out of the path of an onrushing Indian vehicle."

chicken à la king. Chicken à la king, diced pieces of chicken in a sherry cream sauce, is now available canned, frozen, and even in Army mess halls, a long way from the éclat tables where it was served in the late 19th century. The dish was not invented for a king, as is popularly believed, yet it's hard to pinpoint just whom chicken à la king does honor. Some say that New Yorker Foxhall Keene, self-proclaimed "world's greatest amateur athlete," suggested the concoction to a chef at Delmonico's. Of the numerous stories surrounding the dish's creation the most reliable seems to be that of the famous Claridge's Hotel in London. Claridge's claimed that the dish was invented by its chef to honor J. R. Keene, whose horse had won the Grand Prix in 1881. Perhaps J. R. passed on the recipe to his son, the peerless Fox-hall. At any rate, the Keenes did not hold public interest long enough, and the *Keene* in *Chicken à la Keene* eventually became *king.*

chicken feed. Chickens were fed grain too poor for any other use by American pioneers, and these pieces of poor-quality grain had to be small so the chickens could swallow them. This obviously suggested the contemptuous term *chicken feed* for small change (pennies, nickels, and dimes) to riverboat gamblers fleecing small-town suckers. The first inprint mention of the expression is in *Colonel [Davy] Crockett's Exploits* (1836): "I stood looking on, seeing him pick up chicken feed from the green horns." By extension, *chicken feed* has come to mean any small or insignificant amount of money, and even (rarely today) misleading information deliberately supplied or leaked by a government to spies employed by another government.

chicken guts. A humorous term for the gold trim on the cuffs of Confederate uniforms during the Civil War. Also a name used by children for the symbol "&," the ampersand.

chickenhearted; chicken-livered. Not nearly a new expression, *chickenhearted* is first recorded in a 1681 poem by John Dryden: "Where 'tis agreed by bullies chickenhearted/ To fight the ladies first, and then be parted." *Chicken-heart,* for a heart, or courage, as weak as a chicken's, is first attested in 1602. *Chicken-livered* is a variant of the term, first recorded in America in 1857.

a chicken in every pot. Often attributed to Herbert Hoover, this synonym for prosperity was, indeed, a Republican campaign slogan during the election of 1932—a ridiculous one that helped the Demo crats more than the Republicans, with the Great Depression gripping the land. The words can actually be traced to Henry IV of France and his vow on being crowned king in 1589: "If God grants me the usual length of life, I hope to make France so prosperous that every peasant will have a chicken in his pot on Sunday." Assassinated in 1610 when only 57, Henry wasn't able to provide such prosperity.

chicken Marengo. Napoleon's chef invented chicken Marengo at the Battle of Marengo in Lombardy during the Italian campaign, the quite exact date being two o'clock in the afternoon of June 14, 1800. Having

no butter on hand, the resourceful but anonymous chef sautéed the chicken in the local olive oil, adding the sauce consisting of tomatoes, herbs, mushrooms, and white wine.

chicken pulling. A game of Mexican origin played by U.S. cowboys that consisted of burying a live chicken in soft ground up to its neck, the players riding by at a gallop and attempting to pick the chicken out of the ground, usually breaking its neck in the process. The game, also called pulling the chicken, fortunately isn't played much anymore, if at all.

chicken ranch. Unlike most sexual euphemisms, this syno-nym for "a brothel" takes its name from a real place. The original Chicken Ranch was a bordello in Gilbert, Texas, early in this century, so named because poor farmer clients often paid for their visits with chickens. It is celebrated in the play *The Best Little Whore house in Texas.*

chicken scratch; crow tracks. These are Americanisms for illegible handwriting. *Chicken scratch* is first recorded in 1956 but is probably much older, while *crow tracks* dates back to at least 1875. Variations are *hen tracks* and *turkey tracks.*

chickenshit. Petty rules, especially in the Army, probably had been called chickenshit before the first recorded use of the expression in this sense in the 1930s. The early Canadian term *chickenshit* for "information from a superior officer" may be the source for the term.

chick pea. *Chick pea* came into English in the 16th century from the French *pois chiche* for the vegetable and was originally called the *chiche pea,* until people began to confuse the word *chiche* with *chick.* *Cicer arietium* is also known as the *chick bean.* The word has nothing to do with the *chick* of *chicken,* as is often claimed.

chili pepper. The pungent pods of *Capsicum annuum longum* and several other species are named after the Nahuatl *chilli,* meaning the same. *Chilli,* in turn, derives from a Nahuatl word meaning "sharp" or "pointed," because it is so pungent or biting to the tongue. Both "hot" and "sweet" varieties of garden peppers belong to the *Capsicum* genus native to tropical America. They are no relation to the condiment pepper, which is made from the berries of a climbing shrub of the *Piper* genus. Hottest of the hot chili peppers is the *habanero* variety, which is said to cause slight, temporary deafness—so you don't hear your screams when you eat them, some people believe.

chitterlings. Hog intestines made into a popular Southern dish; usually pronounced *chitlins.*

chocolate mousse. One theory has it that this dessert was invented by French artist Henri de Toulouse-Lautrec a century ago. Lautrec gave it the witty name *chocolate mayonnaise,* but this was changed to chocolate *mousse,* ("foam," "lather") over the years.

choke-pear; pears of agony. The choke-pear, whose name also became the synonym for "a severe reproof " in the 16th century, has to be among the most perverse instruments of torture man has invented. Named after the indigestible pear called a choke pear, it was "of iron, shaped like a pear" and originally "used in Holland" by robbers. According to an early source: "This iron pear they forced into the mouths of persons from whom they intended to extort money; and of turning a key, certain interior springs thrust forth a number of points, in all directions, which so enlarged it, that it could not be taken from the mouth: and the iron, being case-hardened, could not be filed; the only methods of getting rid of it were either by cutting the mouth, or advertising a reward for the key. These pears were also called pears of agony."

choke pear; chokecherry. Because of its rough, astringent taste, which could make a person choke, this fruit was called a choke pear. Later the term was applied, figuratively, to anything that stopped someone from speaking, such as biting sarcasm or an unanswerable argument. The wild black cherry is sometimes called the *chokecherry* for similar reasons, and there is a berry called the *chokeberry*.

chop suey. Chop suey isn't native to China; in fact, most accounts of its origin say that the dish was invented in America. The widely accepted theory, advanced by Herbert Asbury in his *Gangs of New York* (1928), makes the tasty melange the brainchild of a San Francisco dishwasher, though the Chinese dishwasher is sometimes promoted to a "cook in a California gold mining camp." I've traced the term's invention, however, to 1896, when it was concocted in New York by Chinese ambassador Li Hung-chang's chef, who tried to devise a dish appealing to both American and Chinese tastes. Since the ambassador had three chefs, it's hard to say which one invented chop suey. The name has nothing to do with the English word "chop," deriving instead from the Cantonese dialect *shap sui,* which means "pieces of mixed bits," *sui* being the Chinese for "bits." The chef who invented it took left over pieces of pork and chicken and cooked them together with bean sprouts, green peppers, mushrooms, and seasonings in a gravy, serving it with rice and soy sauce.

chopped liver. Said of something or someone trivial. First recorded in a famous line of American comedian Jimmy Durante: "Now that ain't chopped liver!" Often heard today in the half-humorous complaint "What am I, chopped liver?"

chow. *Ch'ao,* the Mandarin Chinese for "to fry or cook," probably gives us the word *chow,* an Americanism first recorded in the 1850s in California, where there were many Chinese laborers and cooks working on the railroads.

chowder. *Chowder* derives from the French *chaudière,* stew pot, the word brought to the New World by Breton fishermen who settled the Maritime Provinces of Canada. The soup called a clam chowder is made with milk, vegetables, and clams in Maine and Massachusetts, this being the famous New England clam chowder. But in Rhode Island and as far away as New York, it often is made with water, vegetables, tomatoes, and clams, this called Manhattan clam chowder. The two schools are not at all tolerant of each other. One Maine legislator, in fact, introduced a bill making it *illegal* to add tomatoes to chowder within the state of Maine, the penalty being that the offender dig up a barrel of clams at high tide.

chowderhead. According to one theory, neither clam chowder nor any other chowder has anything to do with this expression, used to mean a dolt or a stupid, clumsy person. *Chowderhead,* this theory holds, is a mispronunciation of *cholterhead,* which dates back to the 16th century and is derived from the older term *jolthead.* Unfortunately, we're all a bunch of chowderheads when it comes to the origins of *jolthead.*

cider. That cider was originally hard cider—that is, a fermented alcoholic drink—is witnessed by the derivation of the word, which came into English, via French (*cidre*), from the Latin word *sicera,* which comes from the Hebrew *shekar,* "strong drink." General William Henry Harrison of "Old Tippecanoe and Tyler, too" fame (he was called Tippecanoe because he won a battle against Indians at Tippecanoe River), was also known as the "log cabin and hard cider candidate" when he defeated Martin Van Buren for the presidency in 1840. As a campaign song put it:

> Let Van from his cooler of silver wine drink
> And lounge on his silken settee.
> Our man on a log-cabin bench can recline;
> Content with hard cider is he!

cinnamon. Cinnamon was called *Kinnamomon* by the Greeks, who may have adapted the word from an earlier Semitic one. The bark of the tropical cinnamon tree (*Cinnamonum zeylamium*) yields cinnamon, which has been used as a spice for thousands of years. Most of it comes from Malaya and Indonesia, and the Arabs, seeking to keep their monopoly on trading it, concocted some incredible tales about its harvesting. The Greek historian Herodotus repeated this story:

> What they say is that the dry sticks
> . . . are brought by
> large birds which carry them to their nests, made of
> mud, on mountain precipices which no man can climb,
> and that the method the Arabians have invented for
> getting hold of them is to cut up the bodies of dead
> oxen, or donkeys, or other animals, into very large
> joints which they carry to the spot in question and leave
> on the ground near the nests. They then retire to a safe
> distance and the birds fly down and carry off the joints
> of meat to their nests, which, not being strong enough
> to bear the weight, break, and fall to the ground. Then
> the men come along and pick up the cinnamon, which is . . .
> exported to other countries.

clam chowder. By New England definition clam chowder is a dish made with clams, vegetables and *milk*—never with a tomato base. Manhattan clam chowder, however, is *always* made with tomatoes. This great American gastronomic controversy became national news in February 1939 when Assemblyman James Seeder introduced a bill into the Maine legislature making the use of tomatoes in clam chowder illegal. The punishment his unenacted bill specified: Make any offender harvest two bushels of clams at high tide. *See* CHOWDER.

clean as a peeled egg. This phrase refers to a cooked egg with its shell removed, which is of course a shiny white.

climb a sour apple tree. First recorded in the early 1900s but probably older, *go climb a sour apple tree* means "go to blazes, go to hell." It is an Americanism that is still occasionally heard.

cocktail. There are well over 50 theories as to the word *cocktail's* origin, H. L. Mencken alone presenting seven plausible ones in his *American Language.* These include a derivation from the French *coquetier,* "an egg cup," in which the drink was supposedly first served in 1800; from *coquetel,* "a mixed drink of the French Revolution period"; from the English *cock-ale,* "fed to fighting cocks"; from *cocktailings,* "the last of several liquors mixed together"; and from a toast to that cock that after a cockfight had the most feathers left in its tail. Just as reliable as any of these guesses is the old folktale that Aztec King Axolotl VIII's daughter Octel or Xochitl concocted the first cocktail; or, in another version, that an Aztec noble sent his emperor a drink made of cactus juice by his daughter, the emperor enjoying it so much that he married the girl and called the drink by

her name—again Octel or Xochitl. According to this story, General Scott's soldiers are supposed to have brought the drink back to America centuries later. Suffice it to say that the origin of the word, first printed in 1806, is really unknown.

cocktail party. Cocktail parties have been traced back as far as ancient Athens, where you could drop by a neighbor's early in the evening with your own goatskin of wine and be treated to a variety of "provocatives to drinking" that included caviar, oysters, shrimp, cheese, and even marinated octopus and roasted grasshoppers. The literary cocktail party is a creature of recent times, possibly evolving from the literary dinner parties so popular in the 19th century. Sherwood Anderson died of peritonitis and its complications after swallowing a toothpick with an hors d'oeuvre at a cocktail party.

coconut crab; robber crab. The large robber crab or coconut crab (Birgus latro) of the Pacific islands is closely related to hermit crabs, but has given up carrying a portable dwelling and developed a permanent hard-plated shell. Called the *coconut crab* because it climbs palm trees to get the fruit, it is named the *robber crab* for an entirely different reason. After chasing another crab, *Cardisoma,* into its hole in the ground, the robber crab threatens to enter. When *Cardisoma* thrusts out its big claw to guard the entrance, the robber crab seizes it, twists it off, and scuttles off to enjoy a gourmet feast.

coconut; copra. Safe in its buoyant, waterproof pod, the coconut sailed the high seas from southern Asia in prehistoric times and was propagated and cultivated throughout tropical regions. But it wasn't given its present name until the late 15th century, when Portuguese explorers came upon it in the Indian Ocean islands and fancied that the little indentations at the base of the nut looked like eyes. Thinking that these three "eyes" gave the nut the look of a grinning face, they named it the *coconut,* coco being the Portuguese word for "a grinning face." The nut deserves a better appellation, having been "the fruit of life" for ages, providing people with food, drink, oil, medicines, fuel, and even bowls, not to mention the many uses of the 60-to 100-foot tree it grows on. Copra, important to the plot of many a South Sea tale, is the dried meat of coconuts that oil is pressed from, and *coconut* itself is slang for "a head," which takes the word back to its origins. *Copra* derives from the Hindu *Rhopra* for coconut.

cod; you can't cod me. Experts have suggested that *cod* might derive from an old Danish word for "bag" (because it was said to be a "bag fish," in reference to its shape), but its origin must be marked unknown due to lack of evidence, even though the word has been wiThus at least since the 14th century. The North Atlantic cod *(Gadus morrhua),* reaching a length of up to three feet and a weight of up to 50 pounds, has long been one of the most important fish of commerce *(see* codfish aristocracy). It is called the *sacred cod* because it is said to be the fish that Christ multiplied and fed to the multitude. According to one early-19th-century writer: "Even today the marks of His thumbs and forefingers are plainly visible on the codfish. His Satanic majesty stood by and said he, too, could multiply fish and feed multitudes. Reaching for one of the fish it wriggled and slid down his red-hot fingers, burning two black stripes down its side and thus clearly differentiating the haddock from the sacred cod. These markings, in actual practice, do distinguish one fish from another." *You can't cod me* means "You can't get a rise out of me, you won't make me rise to the bait like a codfish."

codfish aristocracy.

> Of all the fish that swim or swish
> In ocean's deep autocracy,
> There's none possesses such haughtiness
> As the codfish aristocracy.
>
> —Wallace Irwin

It's hard to think of any group haughtier than the Cabots and Lowells (who spoke only to God, according to another old poem), but the Boston nouveau riche who made their money from the cod-fishing industry in the late 18th and early 19th century apparently gave a grand imitation of them. At any rate, they were disliked enough to inspire the derogatory expression *codfish aristocracy,* for "any pretentious, newly rich person."

coffee. *Coffee* was introduced to England from Turkey, where it was called *qahwah,* pronounced *kahveh,* a word that apparently first meant some kind of wine and derived from a verb meaning "to have no appetite." The word came to England, per-haps from the *Italian caffè,* in about 1600. At first coffee's reputation wasn't good, one early English traveler warning that it "intoxicated the brain." It has had widely varying reviews since.

coffee as a secret weapon. Today's Starbucks drinkers would not appreciate the potent coffee Honoré de Balzac liked to drink. The French author liked to begin work at midnight and write for 18 hours at a stretch. Often, he kept himself awake by drinking 30 cups of coffee a night, and he was so poor while writing the *Comédie Humaine* that he had to lock himself up in a secret writing room to hide from creditors. The caffeine-loaded sludgelike

coffee he drank stimulated his mind, he claimed; after he drank it ideas "poured out like the regiments of the Grand Army over the battlefield."

cold fish. An emotionally cold, impassive person, either a man or a woman. The expression, first recorded in the early 1920s in the U.S., can also mean a sexually cold or frigid person.

coleslaw; hot slaw. The word is *coleslaw,* not *cold slaw,* and isn't so named because the dish is served cold. An American-ism of Dutch origin, *coleslaw* derives from the Dutch *koolsla,* composed of *kool,* "cabbage," plus *sla,* "salad." First recorded in 1792, it must be older, as Dutch farmers on Long Island cultivated the first cabbage in America long before this. Though there is no *cold slaw,* there is a *hot slaw,* the word for this dish first recorded in 1870.

cook his (her) goose. The Mad King of Sweden, Eric XIV, was supposedly so enraged because residents of a medieval town he had attacked hung out a goose, a symbol of stupidity, to "slyghte his forces" that he told the residents "[I will] cook your goose" and proceeded to burn the town to the ground. This story is generally disregarded, because Mad King Eric supposedly avenged his insult in about 1560 and the expression *cook his goose*—"to put an end to, ruin"—isn't recorded until 1851. Attempts have been made to relate the phrase to the old Greek fable of the goose that laid the golden eggs. The peasant couple to whom that goose belonged, you'll remember, killed it (and perhaps cooked it later) because they were eager to get at the golden eggs within its body, which turned out to be undeveloped in any case. The first recorded use of the phrase *cook his goose* is in a London street ballad condemning "Papal Aggression" when Pope Pius IX tried to strengthen the power of the Catholic church in England with his appointment of Nicholas Wiseman as English cardinal:

> If they come here we'll cook their goose,
> The Pope and Cardinal Wiseman.

cookin' with gas. Efficient gas ranges were common in the United States before World War I, models including the 1912 Lindemann with four burners, a broiler, and an oven for $57. But starting in the 1930s, the U.S. gas industry began a public relations campaign trying to convince consumers to use gas rather than increasingly popular electric ranges. This resulted in the widely used saying *now you're cookin' with gas,* "now you've got the right idea, are on the right track," etc. The same is true of the synonym *to cook on the front burner* ("Brother, you're cookin' on the front burner").

cool as a cucumber. It took scientists with thermometers until 1970 to find out what has been folk knowledge for centuries—that cucumbers are indeed cool, so much so that the inside of a field cucumber on a warm day registers about 20 degrees cooler than the outside air. The belief is ancient, but was first put on paper by Francis Beaumont and John Fletcher in their play *Cupid's Revenge* (1610), when they referred to certain women "as cold as cucumbers." The metaphor describes anyone self-possessed and unemotional. *Cucumber,* which derives from the Latin *cucumir,* was considered "bookish" and commonly pronounced *cowcumber* in England in the early 19th century, the way Sara Gamp said it in Dickens's *Martin Chuzzlewit.* Roman emperor Tiberius is said to have enjoyed the "fruits" so much that he ordered them served to him every day, even though they had to be grown in green houses out of season.

coot stew. A few generations ago people actually enjoyed this dish. Wrote one feisty Yankee world traveler in the late 19th century: "Frederick's pressed duck at the Tour d'Argent isn't bad, but it can't hold a candle to coot stew." There is a real recipe for coot stew, but the anonymous old Maine recipe for it is more famous: "Place the bird in a kettle of water with a red building brick free of mortar and blemishes. Parboil that coot and brick together for three hours. Pour off the water, fill the kettle, and again parboil three hours.

Once more throw off the water, refill the kettle, and this time let the coot and brick sim-mer together over-night. In the morning throw away the coot and eat the brick."

corn coffee. A substitute coffee made from parched corn and other ingredients. In 1844, an American traveler wrote: "The supper con-sisted of coffee made of burnt acorns and maize . . . He advised us to drink some of this corn coffee." The traveler didn't like it very much.

corn dodger. Usually a fried or baked corn bread cake, though it can be boiled. In fact, one theory has it that the name *dodger* for this southern treat comes from the boil-ing water moving them around in the pot.

corned beef. There is of course no corn in corned beef. The *corned* here is for the corns, or grains, of salt used in preparing this "salted beef."

corn in Egypt. An expression that has come to mean anything that can be purchased relatively cheaply in abundance. The Bible is the origin of the expression (Gen. 42:2): "And he said, behold, I have heard that there is corn in Egypt; get you down hither, and buy us from thence; that we may live, and not die."

corn; maize. When in Keats's "Ode to a Nightingale" a home-sick Ruth stands "in tears amid the alien corn" (the phrase is Keats's own and not from the King James Bible), she is standing in a field of wheat or rye, any grain but New World corn. The English have always used the word corn to describe all grains used for food and never specifically for the grain that built the Mayan and Incan empires. Corn derives from the Old Teutonic *kurnom,* which is akin to *granum,* the Latin word for grain. *Kurnom* eventually became the Old Saxon *korn* and then *corn* in Old English. The semantic con-fusion arose when English settlers in America named corn on the cob "Indian corn" soon after Squanto brought ears to the starving Puritan colony in Massachusetts; the set-tlers then dropped the cumbrous quali-fying adjective "Indian" over the years.

The British call our "corn" *maize,* a word that derives from the Spanish *maiz,* which has its ori-gins in *mahiz,* a Carib be an Indian tribe's name for the plant. But while "corn" is the most valuable food plant native to the New World and has a fascinating history and mani-fold uses (employed in more than 600 products, it may even have been used as a binding for this book), it is still little known in Europe. This is perhaps because most corn loses some 90 percent of its sugar con-tent an hour after harvesting and can't survive a transatlantic voyage without losing practically all its taste, though today there are new varieties that hold their sugar much longer.

Cornelian cherry. The berries of several dogwood species are edible, but those of the Cornelian cherry (*Cornus mas*) have the longest history as a food. Called "cornet plums" in England, this tree's scarlet berries were once used to make preserves, tarts, and drinks, and were even packed in brine to be used like olives. In addition, the Cornelian cherry has exceedingly hard wood that gives more heat than most firewoods, and is said to have been used to build the Trojan horse. Its bark yields the red dye used for the traditional Turkish fez, and the berries of a dwarf form of it (*Cornus sericea*) were believed by the Scottish Highlanders to create appetite, inspiring them to name the plant *Lus-a-chraois,* Gaelic for "plant of gluttony." Like all species of dogwood, the Cornelian cherry's bark is rich in tannin and has been used medicinally (just as the bark of the flowering dogwood, *Cornus florida,* was used as a substitute for quinine). Virgil in the *Aeneid* tells how Aeneas, landing in Thrace, pulls up several Cornelian cherry bushes and finds their roots dripping blood. Groans come from the hole and a voice cries out that his murdered kinsman Polydorus is buried there. Ae-neas then performs funeral rites so that the spirit of Polydorus can rest in peace. *See* DOGWOOD TREE.

corn pone. *Corn pone* is a famous southern American corn-meal cake or bread, defined by *Bartlett* in 1859 as "a superior type of corn bread, made with milk and eggs and cooked in a pan." It is often called "corn bread." *Cornpone* has also come to be a derogatory term for someone or something rural and unsophisticated: "That's a cornpone story." The word *pone* comes from the Powhatan Indian word *apan,* something baked.

couch potato. A phrase from a pun. *Couch potato* means a lazy, inactive person who does little else in leisiure time save lie on the couch watching TV. As for the punning derivation of *couch potato,* first came the slang term boob tube for television, recorded in 1963. Someone who watched too much of the *boob tube* was shortly after dubbed a "boob-tuber." *Boob tuber* suggested the potato, a plant tuber, to Tom Iacino of Pasadena, California, in 1976, and he invented the term *couch potato,* which he registered as a trademark eight years later. Soon after his inventive punning, Iacino and some friends formed a club called the Couch Potatoes, which appeared in the 1979 Pasadena Doo Dah Parade, in which they lay on couches watching TV while their fl oat was pulled through the streets. Little remained but for cartoonist Robert Armstrong to draw the familiar image of a couch potato—a potato sprawled out on a couch watching TV—for his book *Dr. Spudd's Etiquette for the Couch Potato* (1982).

crabs in a bucket. The words of a resident in a New York City housing project where feuds and crime have caused death and suffering (*New York Times,* August 23, 2004): "It's crabs in a bucket out here. They're all climbing up over each other to get out, but meanwhile they're all pulling each other back down." Crabs are commonly stored in a bushel basket or bucket when caught while crabbing.

cranberry. This berry grows wild in the marshlands favored by cranes, which leads some experts to trace it to the Low German word *kraanbere.* However, since the word is recorded in America as early as 1647—a time when it is unlikely that Low German terms would have much currency here—it could be that Americans coined the word independently, noting themselves that the berry grew where cranes lived.

crisp. *Crisp* is British slang for what Americans call a potato chip. But in British English *crisp* also means to die by arson, as in "He was crisped in that big fire." *Crisp bread* are crackers popular as a bread substitute for dieters.

croissant. Croissants were first made by the Viennese in 1689 to celebrate the lifting of the siege of Vienna by the Turks. The Viennese called the rich crescent-shaped rolls *Hornchen,* "a crescent-shaped object," but today the French *croissant,* a translation of *Hornchen,* is their most common name throughout the world.

crop. A crop was originally the top or head of a plant; these were gathered during the harvest, of course, and came to be the general name for what was collected, the crop.

crud. An Americanism dating back to the early 1920s in army use, *crud* doesn't come directly from the Middle English *crudd,* for "coagulated solids of milk, or curds," even though Shakespeare used the word *crudy* in this sense. It probably derives from the mispronunciation of the word *curdled* as *cruddled,* anything curdled or cruddled being undesirable crud. The word first described semen sticking to the body or clothes after sexual intercourse, and was probably so named for this, but is now used mainly as a synonym for feces, or, even more commonly, for "anything dirty, inferior, worthless, ugly, or disgusting."

crowder. A variety of black-eyed pea that grows crowded together in the pod; in his diary, George Washington records growing them, and they are widely grown today.

cry over spilt milk. Canadian humorist Thomas C. Haliburton, whose Down East humor strongly influenced American literature, had a friend say this to his famous character Sam Slick, a shrewd Yankee peddler, in *The Clockmaker; or the Sayings and Doings of Samuel Slick of Slickville* (1836). "What's done, Sam, can't be helped, there is no use cryin' over spilt milk" were the exact words. This is the first use of the expression in print, though to *cry over spilt milk* seems homely enough to be of much older origin. It expresses, of course, the folly of vain regret, meaning "to grieve over something beyond saving," something you can't do anything about. Haliburton, a Canadian jurist, later returned to England and became a member of Parliament.

Cuban sandwich. A name, generally confined to Florida, for a submarine or hero sandwich. The sandwich, often grilled, seems to have been introduced in the early 1970s.

cupcake. Damon Runyon coined this word for a pretty young girl from "cake." It first appeared in a short story he wrote for *Collier's Magazine* (May 6, 1939). Other words he coined for a pretty young thing are *honeysuckle, nasturtium, pancake,* and *gorgeous.*

cuppa. A cup of tea or coffee. Originally British slang, but now also used in the United States. First recorded in a 1925 P. G. Wodehouse story.

curry favor. These words are literally meaningless. What does currying, or brushing, favour have to do with bootlicking, or ingratiating oneself by flattery? The expression shows that a mistake repeated often enough can become standard usage. *Favor* here is a corruption of *Fauvel.* Fauvel was a fallow-colored or chestnut horse in the early 14th-century satirical poem *Roman de Fauvel.* The equine hero of this popular French allegory symbolized cunning duplicity; thus cunning people who resorted to insincere flattery in order to gain someone's favor were said to curry Fauvel, to groom or brush the rascally fallowcolored horse so that he would look kindly on them and perhaps impart to them his powers of duplicity. *Fauvel* came to be spelled *favel* in English. But because *favel* sounded like *favor* to Englishmen and because the idea of gaining someone's favor is the essence of the phrase, the proverbial expression became *curry favor.*

cut up (or split) the melon. This means to divide the spoils or profits of any kind, each person getting a slice of the tasty melon, or profits. Surprisingly, it is a relatively recent term, dating back only to 1906 or so, when it arose as Wall Street jargon for the distribution of extra, unexpected dividends to stockholders.

D

daily bread. The essentials, the food or money needed in order to live. The common term is from the Lord's Prayer (Matt. 6:9): ". . . Give us this day our daily bread."

Danish pastry. Often shortened to *Danish*, this sweet buttery pastry made with raised dough was named not after a country but for the Danish baker, who made them at Gertner's restaurant in Manhattan a century ago. The Danes in Denmark used the expression *Vienna bread* at the time, as they still do.

dark meat; white meat. These were originally American euphemisms for the leg and the breast, respectively, of turkey and other fowl, *leg* and *breast* being embarrassing words in Victorian times. The words are still frequently used, but descriptively now and not euphemistically.

date. Date palms from the Mediterranean area were introduced to America by Spanish missionaries in the early 1700s. The fruit of this palm takes its name from the Latin *dactylus,* "finger," as people in ancient times believed it resembled the human finger. The date has been called "the candy that grows on trees" because about half its weight is sugar. Th ousands of acres of date trees grow in California's Coachella Valley. Their large bunches of fruit are wrapped in heavy paper to protect them from insects and moisture, and helicopters periodically hover over the groves to fan away dampness. A merely "average" date palm produces about 100 pounds of fruit a year. In times past, dates were cheaper than grain in some regions, and the tree was said to have 360 uses, ranging from fermented drinks made from its sap to the "cabbage" consisting of the new foliage sprouting from its crown.

Dead Sea fruit. In days past the apple of Sodom was thought to grow along the Dead Sea, the mythical fruit beautiful to be-hold but turning to ashes when touched. From this belief arose the expression Dead *Sea fruit* for something promising that turns out to be worthless, the phrase first recorded in 1868 as the title of a novel but probably older.

delicatessen. A store or department of a store in which many cooked or prepared foods such as cold meats, cheeses, salads, etc., are sold. The word derives directly from the German *delicatessen*, delicacy, which comes ultimately from the Latin *delicatus*, pleasing. Often the short form *deli* is used: "We're having delicatessen [or deli] for dinner."

die for the want of lobster sauce. Vatel, the chef of the French prince de Condé, is said to have killed himself because the lobsters (or fish) he needed for a sauce he was preparing for Louis XIV didn't arrive on time. Thus, *to die for the want of lobster sauce* is said of someone who suffers greatly because of some small disappointment.

dim sum. A Cantonese appetizer whose name translates as "little heart" or "heart's delight."

dine. Meaning to eat, possibly to eat well or to eat "seriously" (not to eat a sandwich, for example), *to dine* originally meant "to eat dinner, the principal meal of the day." In this respect the word is a contradiction, deriving as it does from the Latin *disjunare,* "to breakfast, to eat the *first* meal of the day."

dine with Duke Humphrey. It was popularly believed in days of yore that Humphrey, duke of Gloucester (1391–1447), a man noted for his hospitality, was buried in London's old St. Paul's Cathedral. For many years after his death those poor who remained in the cathedral during dinner hours, or those debtors afraid to leave the sanctuary for fear of imprisonment, were said to be dining with Duke Humphrey. Although the good duke had actually been buried at St. Albans, the expression *to dine with Duke Humphrey* remained linked with St. Paul's and came to mean to go without any dinner at all. It is now solely a literary expression, often found in the novels of Dickens and other great English authors.

dinner on horse back. A famous dinner given by American millionaire C. K. Billings at Louis Sherry's restaurant in 1903. The guests, all men, lounged in the saddle astride horses that had been brought to the ballroom by elevator. The diners ate pheasant from feed bags and drank champagne from large rubber casks. It was said that Billings spent $50,000 for the feast, including the planting of sod on the ballroom floor. A couple of years later, in 1905, millionaire Diamond Jim Brady topped Billings with a dinner he gave for his race horse Gold Heels; it cost over $100,000, including the $60,000 he spent for diamond jewelry for each guest.

doesn't know beans. Boston, home of the "bean eaters," "home of the bean and the cod," may be behind the phrase. Walsh, in his *Handy-book of Literary Curiosities* (1892), says that the American expression originated as a sly dig at Boston's pre-tensions to culture, a hint that Bostonians knew that Boston baked beans were good to eat, that they were made from small white "pea beans"—even if Bostonians knew nothing else. It may also be that the American phrase is a negative rendering of the British saying "he knows how many beans make five"—that is, he is no fool, he's well informed—an expression that probably originated in the days when children learned to count by using beans. But *he doesn't know beans*, "he don't know from nothing," possibly has a much simpler origin that either of these theories. It probably refers to the fact that beans are little things of no great worth, as in the expression "not worth a row (or hill) of beans."

don't make two bites of a cherry. The expression is an old one warning against dividing things too small to be divided, against prolonging for two days jobs that should take only one. It may have some connection with polite European courtiers three centuries ago who acted so daintily in public that they always took two bites to eat a cherry.

donkey meat. It is said that the French highly value, or valued, donkey meat—certainly more so than that of the horse. A dish called *donkey's brains à la diplomate* was supposed to be served at a luncheon given to Napoleon III. However, the *Larousse Gastronomique* says: "We find it difficult to believe in the veracity of this story."

doughnuts. American doughnuts go back to the time of the Pilgrims, who learned to make these "nuts" of fried sweet dough in Holland before coming to the New World. It is to the Pennsylvania Dutch that we owe the hole in the middle of the doughnut, or sinker, as the doughnut is sometimes called.

drinking club. A Greek lyric poet, Anacreon (6th century B.C.), wrote light poems praising wine and love that were imitated by Jonson, Herrick, and other early English bards. A drinking club in London used his name, and its club song, "Anacreon in Heaven," provided the music for Francis Scott Key's "Star-Spangled Banner," the American national anthem.

drinking mash and talking trash. Said of someone drunk for whom liquor is doing the talking, who isn't reasoning properly. "You're drinkin' mash and talkin' trash, man."

drink like a fish. Fish don't intentionally drink water. Most of the water they appear to be drinking while swimming along is actually passing through their gills to supply them with oxygen. But they certainly do *seem* to be drinking continually, many swimming with their mouths open. That is why what has been called an "idiotism" (like "cold as hell") has been a common synonym for drinking excessively, especially alcohol, since at least the early 17th century.

drink off dead Nelson. To drink alcohol copiously and indiscriminately. Lord Horatio Nelson, England's greatest naval hero, was killed at the battle of Trafalgar in 1805, and his body was brought back to England for burial. The fabled hero became the subject of many legends, including one claiming that his body was brought home preserved in rum. This led to the British slang expression *Nelson's blood* for rum and the Canadian expression recorded here, used mainly in Newfoundland.

drunk as a lord. Both *drunk as a lord* and *drunk as a beggar* were coined in the mid 17th century, but only the former expression survives today—perhaps because most drunks like to consider themselves lords rather than beggars. Three hundred years ago there were no class restrictions on drinking in England and anyone could buy enough gin to get drunk on for a penny.

drunk as a skunk. Very drunk. Why a skunk should be especially drunk is unknown to me, but several writers have recorded the definition. It may have something to do with the smell of a human drunk's clothing after a binge, but that is just a guess of my own. The animal does leave a foul odor when it sprays, however, and leaves the victim stinko. Then again maybe it was just the rhyming words *drunk-skunk* that caused all the trouble.

as drunk as David's sow. Very drunk, "beastly drunk." The wife of David Lloyd, "a Welchman who kept an alehouse at Hereford" became known to history as David's sow early in the 17th century. "David," according to one old story, "had a living sow, which was greatly resorted to by the curious; he had also a wife much addicted to drink . . . One day David's wife having taken a cup too much, and being fearful of the consequences [David's wrath], turned out the six-legged sow and lay down to sleep herself sober in the stye. A company coming to see the sow, David ushered them into the stye, exclaiming, 'There is a sow for you! Did any of you ever see such another?,' all the while supposing that the sow had really been there. To which some of the company, seeing the state the woman was in, re- plied, it was the drunkenest sow they had ever beheld; whence the woman was ever after called *David's sow.*"

duxelles sauce. A *duxelles* today is a purée of mushrooms and onions, the tasty sauce once made from a much more elaborate recipe. It was named for the marquis d'Uxelles, employer of the too often ignored chef François Pierre de la Varenne. Varenne's *Le Cuisinier Français* (1651) is a landmark of French cuisine, and his rare pastry book *Le*

Patissier Français has been called the most expensive cookbook in the world. The chef is said to have been trained by those Florentine cooks brought to France by Marie de' Medici, second wife of Henry IV. It is often claimed that these Italians taught the French the art of cooking, but Varenne's cuisine was much more delicate and imaginative than that of his masters; and if anyone can be called the founder of classical French cuisine he deserves the honor. Varenne did not name the *duxelles* after his employer; this was done at a later date when it became customary to honor a man's name in a recipe.

E

eat humble pie. Here is an expression probably born as a pun. The *humble* in this pie has nothing to do etymologically with the word *humble,* "lowly," which is from the Latin *humilis,* "low or slight." Umbles or numbles (from the Latin *lumbulus,* "little loin") were the innards—the heart, liver, and entrails—of deer and were often made into a pie. Sir Walter Scott called this dish "the best," and an old recipe for it (1475) instructed "For to serve a Lord"—but some thought it fit only for servants. When the lord of a manor and his guests dined on venison, the menials ate umble pie made from the innards of the deer. Anyone who ate umble pie was therefore in a position of inferiority—he or she was humbled—and some anonymous punster in the time of William the Conqueror, realizing this, changed *umble pie* to *humble pie,* the pun all the more effective because in several British dialects, especially the Cockney, the *h* is silent and *humble* is pronounced *umble* anyway. So the play upon words gave us the common expression *to eat humble pie,* meaning to suffer humiliation, to apologize, or to abase oneself.

eat dog for another. Various American Indian tribes ate dog meat, and at least one was called *the Dogeaters* by their enemies. When white men sat at Indian councils where dog meat was served, those who didn't relish the comestible could, without offending their host, put a silver dollar on the dish and pass it along, the next man taking the dollar and eating the dog. From this practice arose the American political expression *to eat dog for another.*

eat, drink, and be merry, for tomorrow we die. Brewer tells us that this was "a traditional saying of the Egyptians, who, at their banquets, exhibited a skeleton to the guests to remind them of the brevity of life." *Eat, drink, and be merry* itself, however, appears in Eccles. 8:15: "A man hath no better thing under the sun than to eat, drink and be merry."

eatin' a green 'simmon. The *'simmon* in this 19th-century Americanism is a persimmon, which takes its name from the Cree *pasiminan* (dried fruit). Although the fruit is delicious when thoroughly ripe, a green unripe persimmon is so sour it could make you whistle, which led to the expression *he looks like he's been eatin' a green 'simmon.* On the other hand, ripe persimmons suggested *walking off with the persimmons* (walking off with the prize), which also dates back to the 1850s.

eating rat. During the siege of Paris in 1871, when Prussian troops besieged the city for 135 days, Frenchmen ate labeled rat meat sold at the rat market in the Place de l'Hotel, the rodents costing three francs apiece (as compared to 10 francs for cats). To Parisians who survived the terrible siege, having "eaten rat" became the symbol of their greatest humiliation.

eat'm and beat'm. A humorous name for cafeterias where the food (generally sandwiches and drinks) was left out on tables for customers to choose from, each customer trusted to add up his or her bill honestly from the prices listed. Owners of these places generally agreed that people were quite honest about doing so, despite the cynical name given to such establishments. Nevertheless, few such places were left by the 1980s.

eat me out of house and home. "Stay out of that refrigerator— you'll eat me out of house and home!" An old phrase that may have been coined by Shakespeare in *Henry IV, Part 2.*

eat one's hat. This is an asseveration, as the *O.E.D.* so neatly puts it, "stating one's readiness to do this if an event of which one is certain should not occur." A woman named Miss E. E. Money first recorded the phrase, in 1887, and it is sometimes given as *I'll eat Rowley's hat.* One per sis tent folk etymology has the *hat* here being "a food made of eggs, veal, dates, saffron, salt, and spices" that no one else seems to have heard of.

eat one's words. "God eateth not his word when he hath once spoken" is the first recorded use of this expression meaning "to retreat in a humiliating way"—in a 1571 religious work. There are several instances of people literally eating their words, the earliest occurring in 1370 when the pope sent two delegates to Bernabo Visconti bearing a rolled parchment, informing him that he had been excommunicated. Infuriated, Visconti arrested the delegates and made them eat the parchment, words, leaden seal, and all. I doubt that this suggested *to eat one's own's words,* but it is a good story.

eat something with one toe in the fire. A colorful backwoods expression meaning that something tastes so good one could enjoy eating it even while in extreme pain. "Mmmmmm, this is so good I could eat it with one toe in the fire."

eat the Yank way. To Brits, who have long called Americans Yanks, this phrase means to hold the fork in the right hand, as Americans generally do.

egg cream. No one has identified the genius who first concocted the egg cream, but this New York favorite was invented in the 1920s at a New York soda fountain. There are no eggs and no cream in an egg cream, so it is something of a misnomer. While no exact recipe for one can be given and egg cream lovers all seem to have their own methods and proportions for making one, it is generally agreed that its ingredients must be milk, seltzer from a seltzer bottle, and Fox's U-Bet Chocolate Flavor Syrup.

egg on. The expression *to egg on* has nothing to do with hen's eggs or any kind of eggs. Neither does it derive from Norman invaders pricking Anglo-Saxon prisoners in the buttocks with their *ecgs* ("the points of their spears") when urging them to move faster, as one old story claims. *To egg on* is just a form of the obsolete English verb "to edge": to incite, provoke, encourage, urge on, push someone nearer to the edge. To *egg* someone meant the same as to *edge* someone and was used that way until about 1566, when the expression was first lengthened and became *to egg on.*

egg phrases (a dozen more, ungraded).
as alike as eggs—"We are almost as like as eggs"— Shakespeare, *The Winter's Tale,* 1611.
break an egg in someone's pocket—to spoil someone's plan, 1734.
crush in the egg—to crush at the very beginning, as in crushing rebellion, 1689.
eggshell blond—a bald man—Australian slang, 1945.
find a hair upon an egg—to make a picky criticism— "Critics that spend their eyes to find a hair upon an egg" (1606).
have eggs on the spit—to have business in hand, 1598.
in egg and bird—in youth and maturity, 1711.

put all your eggs in one basket—to risk all on a single venture—" 'Tis the part of a wise man to keep himself today for tomorrow, and not venture all his eggs in one basket," Cervantes, *Don Quixote*, 1605. "Put all your eggs in one basket and WATCH THAT BASKET," Mark Twain, *Pudd'nhead Wilson*, 1894.

take eggs for money—to be fooled with something worthless, 1611.

teach one's grandmother to suck eggs—to lecture one's elders or betters—dates from about 1700 and was originally *to teach one's dame to grope* (handle) *ducks* (1590).

turn up the eggs of the eyes—the whites of the eyes— " The eggs of their eyes were at their highest elevation" (1635).

walk on eggs—to walk warily, 1734.

eggnog. Eggnog is an American invention, the word first recorded at the time of the Revolutionary War. Made of eggs, milk, sugar, spices, and rum or other spirits, it takes its name from the eggs in it and *nog* for "strong ale."

eggplant. Eggplant of course, takes its common name from its supposed resemblance to a large egg in shape. The vegetable is generally known as the aubergine to the English. Its early reputation varied in Europe, where it was thought to induce insanity and was called the "mad apple," but where it was also considered to be an aphrodisiac and, like the tomato, was dubbed the "apple of love." Native to India, the fruits range in size and in color

from purple-black to white. The name *eggplant* is first recorded in 1767 in England, where the first cultivated eggplants were indeed white and shaped like eggs. An earlier folk name for the fruit was "Guinea squash." Vineland, New Jersey, advertises itself as the "Eggplant Capital of the World," and at its annual *Eggplant Festival* serves many eggplant dishes, including an eggplant wine. *See* AUBERGINE.

eggplant Imam Baildi. A favorite Turkish dish featured in several cookbooks which translates as "the eggplant the imam (a Moslem priest or leader) fainted over." According to the old story, an elderly imam married the daughter of a wealthy oil merchant, who brought as her dowry 12 huge man- sized jars of the world's finest olive oil. A famed cook, his bride prepared him a delicious eggplant dish a few days after the wedding. So pleased was he that he ordered her to prepare the dish every day for dinner. For 12 days all went well, but on the 13th day no eggplant graced the table. When the furious imam demanded to know why, his bride explained: "Dear husband, you shall have to purchase me more oil, as I have used all that I brought with me from my father." This financial shock proved too much for the elderly imam who straightaway fainted.

eggs benedict. Oscar of the Waldorf once confirmed the story that *eggs benedict* was invented by a man suffering from a hangover. It seems that early one morning in 1894, Samuel Benedict, a prominent New York socialite, tread softly into the old Waldorf-Astoria Hotel after a night of partying—his head hurt that much. But he had what he thought was the perfect cure for his splitting headache—a breakfast of poached eggs served on buttered toast and topped with bacon and hollandaise sauce. Oscar, the maitre d'hotel, thought this combination excellent, but substituted an English muffin for the toast and ham for the bacon, naming the dish in Benedict's honor. Whether the cure worked or not isn't recorded, and another version of the tale claims that the dish was created between Oscar and New Yorker Mrs. Le Grand Benedict.

elderberry. He who cultivates the elderberry, says an old proverb, will live until an old age and die in his own bed. Amazing properties have long been attributed to the wine and other products made from *Sambucus nigra.* Said 17th-century English herbalist John Evelyn: "If the medicinal properties of the [elderberry] leaves, bark, berries, etc., were thoroughly known I cannot tell what our countrymen could ail for what he would not find a remedy, from every hedge, either for sickness or wounds."

Empress of Desserts. A nickname for the French apple properly called the Calville. This difficult-to-grow apple is so delicious that in the days of the Sun King it was believed to be the tempting apple that grew in the Garden of Eden.

enjoy every sandwich. According to the *New York Times* (January 30, 2006), this phrase was coined by singer-songwriter Warren Zevon (d. 2003) "and is well on its way to becoming the baby-boom mortality mantra."

Escoffier sauce; Escoffier garnish. If one man had to be chosen to epitomize modern gastronomy it would have to be Auguste Escoffier (1847–1935). Escoffier, made a member of the French Legion of Honor in 1920, was renowned as a chef and restaurateur, operating, with César Ritz, the Ritz in Paris, London's Savoy, and the Grand Hotel in Monte Carlo. Author of a number of books on the art of cooking, Escoffier invented both the basic sauce and the chopped, carmelized almond topping for peach melba that bear his name.

Eskimo Pie. Invented in 1919 and originally called an "I Scream Bar," this still- popular chocolate-covered ice-cream bar was manufactured in 1921 by Russell Stover (for whom the well-known chocolate-covered candies are named) and given the trade name Eskimo Pie.

every bean has it black. This old saw means that everyone has faults. It stems from the fact that many varieties of beans have black "eyes."

F

famine food. Food that people wouldn't normally eat but were forced to consume because nothing else was available. The Irish coined the name during the terrible potato famine of the 19th century, when they ate foods like mussels to ward off hunger and starvation. Mussels, of course, are a gourmet food today. The same could be said of the lobster, which early Americans disdained and called a *bug* (still a term used by Maine lobster fishermen). In fact, our ancestors raked up all the windrows of lobsters storm-swept on our shores and used them for fertilizer. *See* LOBSTER

fast food. McDonald's isn't responsible for this term, which dates back to the early 1940s, but fast-food chains have popularized the expression throughout the world. It refers of course to quickly prepared and served foods, relatively inexpensive and often relatively tasteless.

fava bean. The fava bean takes its name from *faba,* the Latin word for "bean." It is often called the broad bean, horse bean, or Windsor bean. Since antiquity this widely grown legume has been known to cause favism in people of African and Mediterranean origin with a certain enzyme deficiency, fava-bean poisoning sometimes proving fatal.

feeding frenzy. Wild, unseemly attention from the media toward someone in the news has aptly been called a feeding frenzy since the 1980s. Feeding frenzies of sharks, which suggested the expression, were so named 30 years or so before this and describe a pack of sharks surrounding and attacking a large wounded fish or whale.

feed the fishes. This old expression has two meanings. In Sicilian criminal circles it means that someone has been murdered, whether his body has been literally weighted down and thrown into the water or not. The expression was used in Mario Puzo's *The Godfather,* when a large fish is delivered to the Godfather's family and someone explains that this is an old Sicilian message from their enemies meaning one of their henchmen "feeds the fishes." In a more humorous vein, dating back over a century, *feed the fishes* means that someone has become seasick and vomited over the ship's rail into the water.

fig. When someone says "I don't care a fig," she isn't referring to the delicious fruit (whether she knows it or not), but to the ancient "Spanish fig," a contemptuous gesture made by thrusting the thumb forth from between the first two fingers. The insult is said to be an invitation to "kiss my ass." The fig takes its English name from the Latin *ficus,* "fig," which became the Provencal *figa.* It figures in a number of phrases of its own. English, for example, features it in various expressions from the euphemistic *fig you* to far worse, and in French *faire la figue* means "to give the obscene finger gesture." The exclamation, *Frig you* has nothing to do with the "fig you" etymology, however, probably deriving from the Old English *frigan,* to love. The distinguished etymologist Laurence Urdang points out in *The Whole Ball of Wax* (1988) that the natural shape of the fig has much to do with its sexual implications: "When one

encounters fresh figs growing or even in a market, it becomes clear why their visual appearance has given rise to so many translinguistic metaphors: Not to mince words, a pair of fresh figs closely resembles in size and configuration, a pair of testicles. Pressed together, they resemble the external parts of the female genitalia." "Nothing is sweeter than figs," Aristophanes wrote. Figs are mentioned in the biblical story of the Garden of Eden, and it was under a Nepal species of fig tree called the Bo that Buddha's revelations came to him. The ancient Egyptians trained apes to gather figs from trees. According to the biblical story (Gen. 3:7), after the Fall, Adam and Eve covered their nakedness with fig leaves (or leaves of the banyan tree). It wasn't until the era of Victorian

prudery, however, that statues in museums were covered with fig leaves. *Fig Sunday* is an old name for Palm Sunday, when figs used to be eaten to commemorate the blasting of the barren fig tree by Jesus when he entered Jerusalem. The Persian king Xerxes boasted that he would invade Greece, thoroughly thrash all the Greek armies, and then feast on the famous fat figs of Attica. Ever since he was soundly defeated by the Greeks in 480 B.C. at the battle of Salamis, *Attic figs* has meant wishful thinking. *See* JUDAS; SYCOPHANT.

finger in the pie. This expression, recorded in 1659, has nothing to do with being meddlesome, as has been suggested. It means simply "to have something to do with, to have a part in something." "Lusatia . . . must needs, forsooth, have her Finger in the Pye" is the first attested use of the words.

first fruits. John Wycliffe mentions *first fruits* in the first translation into English of the whole Bible (1382), specifically in Num. 18:12 with reference to the custom of making offerings to the Lord of the first fruits gathered in a season. Over two centuries passed before the expression was used figuratively to mean "the first products of one's efforts," as in the *first fruits of our labor.*

fish-and-chips. An originally British dish consisting of fish fried in batter and served with French fries (chips). The delectable dish is no longer served wrapped in newspaper, as it was traditionally. Cod used to be the fish most used by the British in their *fish n' chips*, but haddock and hake are probably more common today. There is now at least one fish n' chips fast food chain.

flower; flour. In Anglo-Saxon times the word for flower was *blossom;* this changed after the Normans conquered England in 1066, and their *fleur* became the English *flower.* However, all three words have the same common ancestor—the ancient Indo-European *blo,* which eventually yielded both *blossom* and *flower. Flour,* the finely ground meal of any grain, is just a specialized use of the word *flower.* In fact, *flower* and *flour* were used interchangeably until the 19th century, as in Milton's *Paradise Lost,* where we find the line "O flours that never will in other climate grow." In French *fleur de farine* is the flower or finest part of the grain meal. Still used today and one of the longest-lived modern-day slogans, the phrase *say it with flowers* was coined for the Society of American Florists in 1917 by plantsman Patrick F. O'Keefe (1872–1934). *Cut flowers* is an old term for flowers cut from the garden for bouquets or display. A visitor once asked George Bernard Shaw why he kept no vases of cut flowers. "I thought you were so fond of flowers," he said. "So I am," Shaw retorted. "I'm very fond of children too. But I don't cut off their heads and stick them in pots all over the house." According to tradition, Saint Elizabeth of Hungary gave so much food to the poor that her own house hold didn't eat well. Her husband suspected this and when he saw her leaving the house one day with her apron full of something, he demanded to know what she carried. "Only flowers, my lord," Elizabeth said, and God saved her from her lie by changing the loaves of bread in her apron to flowers. *See* BLOSSOM.

foie gras; stuffed as a goose; fed up. *Foie gras* literally means "fat liver" in French. Despite its unappetizing name, it has been considered a royal dish from earliest times, the most desirable and expensive of all the patés. The making of foie gras is nothing to be talked about while eating it. Traditionally, a goose was tied down firmly so that it could move only its neck, and six times a day "crammers" used their middle fingers to push into the throats of these geese a thick paste made of buckwheat flour, chestnut flour, and stewed maize. Today the process is hardly more humane. When about six months old, those birds fated for foie gras are crammed into wooden cages along with plentiful food and water. There they would eventually eat themselves to death by suffocation if their keepers did not slaughter them and remove their swollen livers after about six weeks. At that time they're so fat they can barely move, having gorged themselves on over 70 pounds of food. It is said that the term FED UP derives from this cruel practice, though there is no hard evidence of the derivation. *Stuffed as a goose* might more likely derive from the sight of a stuffed goose on a Christmas dinner table. English clergyman and wit Sydney Smith (1771–1845), among others, has been credited with the famous bon mot "My idea of heaven is eating paté de foie gras to the sound of trumpets."

foodie. A foodie, in recent slang, is a gourmand, someone who is a lover of good food. The new word is not widely recorded, but it certainly is widely used. I've never heard it used in the gourmand sense of "a gluttonous eater."

forbidden fruit. An ancient phrase that has its origins in Gen. 3:3, although the exact words are not found there: "But of the fruit of the tree which is in the midst of the garden, God hath said, Ye shall not eat of it, neither shall ye touch it, lest ye die." Figuratively, *forbidden fruit* is usually used to describe a tempting but forbidden person or thing.

fortune cookies. The cookie with a fortune inside was invented in 1918 by David Jung, a contemporary Chinese immigrant who had established Los Angeles's Hong Kong Noodle Company. Jung got the idea after noting how bored customers got while waiting for their orders in Chinese restaurants. He employed a Presbyterian minister (the first fortune cookie author!) to write condensations of biblical messages and later hired Marie Raine, the wife of one of his salesmen, who became the Shakespeare of fortune cookies, writing thousands of classic fortunes such as "Your feet shall walk upon a plush carpet of contentment." The Hong Kong Noodle Company is still in business, as are hundreds of other fortune cookie "publishers." Notable ones include Misfortune Cookies of Los Angeles: "Look forward to love and marriage, but not with the same person." Today fortune cookies are of course served at the end of a meal.

fox grape. *The Theatre of Plants* (1640) by John Parkinson in-forms us that "The Foxe Grape . . . is white, but smelleth and tasteth like unto a Foxe," which is presumably why the American grape is so named. There are two species of wild fox grapes, the northern (*Vitis labrusca*, which is the source of the cultivated Concord grape and other varieties) and the southern (*Vitis rotundifolia*, which is the source of the scuppernong). The wine term *foxy* refers to the pungent fruity flavor of Concord wine and other wines made from native American grapes, these wines reminiscent of jelly or jam to many people. *See* NORTHERN FOX GRAPE.

frankenfood. Genetically engineered fruits and vegetables, such as new strains of corn and tomatoes. The expression takes its name from the idealistic German scientist Baron Frankenstein in Mary Shelley's novel *Frankenstein, or the Modern Prometheus* (1818). Frankenstein, of course, engineered a monster who later turned upon his creator. *Frankenfood* was coined by Paul Lewis, a Boston College English professor, the word first appearing in print in a letter he wrote to the New York Times on June 28, 1992. According to Anne H. Soukhanov in Word Watch (1995), Lewis "coined *Frankenfood* in the second week of June 1992," a few weeks before his *Times* letter. His letter read in part: "Ever since Mary Shelley's baron rolled his improved human out of the lab, scientists have been bringing such good things to life. If they want to sell us Frankenfood, perhaps it's time to gather the villagers, light some torches, and head to the castle."

frankfurter; frank. The frankfurter is named after Frankfurt, Germany, where it was first made centuries ago. Frankfurt itself was so named because it was the "ford of the Franks," the place from which the Franks set out on their raids. The frankfurter seems to have been introduced to the U.S. in St. Louis in about 1880 by Antoine Feuchtwanger, an immigrant from Frankfurt. *Frank for frankfurter* isn't recorded until the 1920s. Franks are also called hot dogs and New York tube steaks. *See* HAMBURGER. Many youngsters think McDonald's invented them, but they were conceived in Belgium toward the middle of the 19th century. From there the Belgian fries spread in popularity to France, and the method of deep frying them soon imported to America, where they are still known under the misnomer French fries.

French toast. In America *French toast* refers to sliced bread soaked in a mixture of eggs and milk before frying the dish golden brown. In England the popular breakfast dish is simply sliced bread fried in bacon fat or butter. The French themselves make it the same way Americans do, calling it *pain perdu* ("lost bread") since the bread is "lost" in the other ingriedents.

from soup to nuts. An American expression for "everything," apparently coined in the late 1920s and obviously based on the menu of a sumptuous meal or banquet at which everything from a first course of soup to a last course of nuts is served. *In the soup* is an Americanism meaning "in trouble."

fruit names. In a delightful *New York Times Magazine* piece (May 30, 2004) Strawberry Saroyan (William Saroyan's granddaughter) tells of four people, including herself, named after fruits: an *Apple*, a *Plum*, and a *Raspberry*. To expand her unique orchard a bit, I would add *Tangerine* (also the title of a pop song), *Cherry, Peaches,* and three famous characters of American literature: Popeye's *Olive*, Herman Melville's *Pip* (short for *pippin*, a delicious apple), and Mark Twain's immortal *Huckleberry Finn*. Drop me a line if you know of any others.

fruit parlor. This English-language borrowing, which is widely used in Japan, means "ice cream parlor." The definition doesn't seem so strange on realizing that the parlors there are named for the fruit used as toppings for ice-cream sundaes, etc.

fudge. Isaac D'Israeli, father of the British prime minister, had an interesting story about the word *fudge,* for "lies or nonsense," in his *Curiosities of Literature* (1791): "There was sir, in our time one Captain Fudge, commander of a merchantman, who upon his return from a voyage, how illfrought soever his ship was, always brought home a good cargo of lies, so much that now aboard ship the sailors, when they hear a great lie told, cry out 'You fudge it!' A notorious liar named Captain Fudge, called "Lying Fudge," did live in 17th-century England. His name, possibly in combination with the German word *futch,* "no good," may well be the source of the word *fudge.* Where the word *fudge* for candy comes from no one seems to know, though it probably dates back to the 19th century.

full of beans, etc. The phrase is used like *full of baloney, full of soup,* and worse, but it usually means someone who is full of energy, high- spir-ited, lively—sometimes in a foolish or silly way. Some say it is a horsey expression, like *full of oats*, going back to the days when horses were fed "horse beans" raised for fodder. The saying, however, is a British one from about 1870 and may derive from an earlier phrase, *full of bread*. Beans, a high- protein food, cer-tainly should make one lively; in fact, they have long been regarded as an aphrodisiac. As an old English ballad, "The Love Bean," put it:

> My love hung limp beneath the leaf
> (O bitter, bitter shame!)
> My heavy heart was full of grief
> Until my lady came.
> She brought a tasty dish to me,
> (O swollen pod and springing seed!)
> My love sprang out right eagerly
> To serve me in my need.

The gas that beans inspire also has something to do with the expres-sion; as the word *prunes*, substi-tuted in the phrase for *beans* some seventy years later, would indicate, both beans and prunes having a laxative effect. In fact, beans were primarily regarded as an aphro-disiac by the ancients because the eructations they caused were thought to produce prodigious erections. But the U.S. Department of Agriculture has recently devel-oped a "gas-less variety," "a clean bean" seed guaranteed not to cause social distress at the dinner table or elsewhere. So bean eaters can now be as full of beans as ever and much less obnoxious, though maybe not as sexy.

fuzzy navel. A peach liqueur and orange juice mixed drink.

G

gammon and spinach. The expression *gammon and spinach* for "nonsense, humbug" is not as familiar today as it was in Dickens's time, when he used it in *David Copperfield*: "What a world of gammon and spinnage it is, though, ain't it!" The phrase, most likely an elaboration of the slang word *gammon*, which meant nonsense or a ridiculous story, is probably patterned on the older phrase *gammon and patter*, the language of London underworld thieves. The nonsense part of it was possibly reinforced by the old nursery rhyme "A Frog He Would A-wooing Go" (1600) heard by millions: "With a rowley powley gammon and spinach/ Heigh ho! says Anthony Rowley."

garlic. Owing to its resemblance to the leek, garlic, the herb that "makes men drink and wink and stink," takes its name from the Old English *garleac: gar*, "spear," and *leac*, "leek." The Romans believed garlic contained magical powers and hung it over their doors to ward off witches, just as some people wear cloves around their necks to protect themselves against colds, diseases, and even vampires. *Pilgarlic* is an interesting word once used to mean a "baldheaded man." It takes its name from the early English *pyllyd garleke*, "peeled garlic," for someone whose head resembles a shiny peeled garlic bulb. Since many bald-headed men were old and pitiful, the word came to take on the meaning of a person regarded with mild contempt or pity, an old fool or someone in a bad way. *See* ONION.

garum; titmuck. It is hard to find anything good to say about the legendary Roman sauce garum, but the ancient Romans loved it. Their garum was made from the putrified guts of fish, blended with fish blood and gills in an open tub, salted heavily, then exposed to the sun, where they were stirred occasionally until the whole mess fermented and herbs were added. At the legendary banquet of the Roman merchant Trimalchio, statuettes of four satyrs in the corners of the room poured vilesmelling garum sauce over fish molded to appear almost alive, to make it seem as if they were swimming in a jelly sea. The only thing comparable to it available today is titmuck, an Eskimo salmon delicacy that ripens in a hole filled with dirt and grass until it decays.

gefilte fish. Hot or cold it is delicious, but the Jewish delicacy, made with many ingredients and traditionally served on Friday nights, is *not* a separate species of fish. Gefilte fish is a kind of fish loaf made of various ground fish, eggs, onions, pepper, salt, and sometimes sugar—every good cook having her or his secret recipe. The "stuffed fish." is more properly called *gefilte fisch* in Yiddish.

gelati. Italian *gelati* have become more popular in America over the past 10 years. *Gelato* is the Italian for ice cream, and the delicacy, which is folded rather than churned when made, has a much higher butter-fat content than any other kind of ice cream.

getting the sugar. A recent expression for diabetes, which is also called the sweet blood.

gimlet. A "healthy" cocktail invented by a naval officer. Anyway, it was a lot healthier than drinking gin neat, which is exactly why Sir. T. O. Gimlette devised the *gimlet* that commemorates him. Gimlette, a British naval surgeon from 1879 to 1917, believed that drinking straight gin harmed the health and impaired the efficiency of naval officers, so he introduced a cocktail that diluted the gin with lime juice. Today the gimlet is made with gin or vodka, sweetened lime juice, and sometimes soda water.

gin and it. A term more familiar with the British than Americans, the gin and it is a type of martini, a drink made of gin and vermouth. The *it* is short for *It*alian vermouth. The drink seems to have been invented in the last 35 years.

gin and tonic. *Tonic,* deriving from the Latin *tonicus,* had only the meaning of "pertaining to tension" when first used in the 17th century. But the word took on the meaning of a medicine that restored the tension or tone of the body, and the first tonic drinks weren't far behind. When people began adding alcohol to such drinks in the 19th century or thereabouts, tonics became the mixers that are today used in concoctions like gin and tonic, enough of which can destroy the tone of the body.

gin rickey. Rickeys can be made of any liquor, carbonated water, and lime juice, but the most famous drink in the family is the gin rickey, invented in about 1895 and named after "a distinguished Washington guzzler of the period," according to H. L. Mencken. Just which Washington Colonel Rickey was so honored is a matter of dispute, however. Several theories have been recorded by Mencken in his *American Language, Supplement 1,* and other sources, but none is generally accepted.

ginseng. Ginseng, which can cost up to $32 an ounce or $512 a pound for a piece of "heaven grade root," has surpassed the cost of even the truffle as a reputed aphrodisiac. In the past it has been sold at $300 an ounce or $4,800 a pound, which is probably the all-time record for a food. One Chinese emperor reputedly paid $10,000 for a perfect man-figure ginseng root, or at least so the story goes. Similarly, it's said that Chairman Mao drank a ginseng tea made from $100-an-ounce ginseng root at least three times a week. At any rate, the herb still sells briskly in Asian markets for $200 a pound and despite the protests of modern pharmacologists, lovers throughout the world cling to the mystique of its so-called super powers. Lovers have been fascinated by the "Man Plant" for more than 5,500 years. The most potent ginseng roots are said to be shaped like a man's body (in fact, the plant takes its name from the Chinese *jen shen,* "man herb") and supposedly even better results are obtained when the root is dug up at midnight during a full moon. The Chinese call ginseng, or *goo-lai-san,* the "elixir of life," "the herb that fills the heart with hilarity," and the "medicine of medicines." An American species of ginseng *(Panax quinquefolium)* is grown and gathered in this country, especially in the Ozarks and Appalachia. Diggers can earn $33 to $44 per pound of dried root, and our largest domestic dealer exports some 70,000 pounds of the herb annually. Such profits are nothing new, however; it is a matter of record that the first American ship to reach China in 1784, Major Samuel Shaw's *Emperor of China,* carried a cargo of the ginseng so dear to Chinese lovers.

give a little sugar. To give a hug or kiss; said especially to a child. "Come over here and give me a little sugar."

glass of wine with the Borgias. It was rumored that Lucretia and Cesare Borgia, the children of Pope Alexander VI, used some secret deadly poison to eliminate their enemies. One never knew whether he was an enemy of the Borgias, so *to have a glass of wine with the Borgias,* or *to dine with the Borgias*

has been proverbial for a great but risky honor since the 16th century. Historians haven't been able to substantiate whether any Borgia was a poisoner, but there is no doubt that some of the Borgias were murderers, the family being a pretty unsavory lot. Sir Max Beerbohm gave the proverb his attention in his *Hosts and Guests*: "I maintain that though you would often in the 15th century have heard the snobbish Roman say, in a would-be off-hand tone, 'I am dining with the Borgias to night,' no Roman was ever able to say, 'I dined last night with the Borgias.'"

go bananas. Go crazy, go wild, act unreasonably. The expression is fairly recent, 50 or so years old as far as is known. It may derive from the saying *to go ape*, bananas being associated with apes, or the phrase may have been suggested by an excited troop of apes or monkeys feeding on bananas.

goat meat. An American euphemism for venison, deer hunted and killed out of the legal hunting season. There are several synonyms, including *goat mutton*.

goober. *Goober*, for "peanut," was not coined in the southern U.S. It originated in Africa as the Bantu *nguba*, for "peanut," and was brought to the America South by African slaves in about 1834. Long a southern dialect term, it has achieved wider currency over the past 70 years. *Pindal*, another word for peanut, comes from the Kongo *npinda*.

good wine needs no bush. Dating back some 2,000 years to ancient Rome, this expression refers to the vine leaves or ivy (honoring Bacchus) frequently depicted on signs outside Roman wine shops or taverns. The Romans continued this custom when they occupied England, where the saying arose that *a good wine needs no bush*, that is, it isn't necessary to advertise a good wine with a bush outside the tavern—its good quality will soon make it known to everyone anyway. Today the words mean generally that "excellent things speak for themselves."

gooseberry fool. Probably the most famous dish made from gooseberries is gooseberry fool, a dessert made of the fruit stewed or scalded, crushed, and mixed with milk, cream, or custard. Some say the *fool* in the dish is a corruption of the French verb *fouler*, "to crush," but this derivation seems to be inconsistent with the use of the word. More probably the dish is simply named after other, older fruit trifles, the use of fool in its name in the sense of "foolish or silly" being suggested by "trifle." In any case, gooseberry fool has been an English favorite since at least 1700. So widely known is the dish that a plant is named after it, the English calling the willow herb *Epilobrium hirsutum* gooseberry fool because its leaves smell like the dessert!

Gorgonzola cheese. The village of Gorgonzola in northern Italy first made this mottled, strong-flavored, semisoft cow cheese that bears its name. Over the years other places in and out of Italy have copied the Gorgonzola recipe, leaving the little village without a monopoly but still with a pride in craftsmanship.

gourmet. The first gourmet was a *groumet*, "a horse groom." The word changed to *gourmet* in French and was applied to grooms and any minor servants in a house hold. Among these servants were boys who tasted wine, and such wine tasters, or *gourmets,* were given the same name when they worked as assistants in wine shops. Eventually the wine-shop *gourmets* became connoisseurs of fine wines and food in general, giving us the *gourmet* we know today. The word is not recorded in English until 1820.

grape; grapefruit; wineberry. Grapefruit (*Citrus paradisi*) resemble grapes only in that they grow in clusters on their trees, but that was sufficient reason to bestow the name upon them, early explorers in Barbados thought. *Grapes* themselves look nothing like their namesakes. Grapes were named for the *grape*, or grapple, the small hook that the French used to harvest them. The English called grapes *wineberries* until they imported the French word toward the end of the 11th century.

grapes of wrath; wrath of grapes. The words *grapes of wrath* are from Julia Ward Howe's "Battle Hymn of the Republic" (1862), which was often sung by Union soldiers in the Civil War: "Mine eyes have seen the glory of the coming of the Lord; / He is trampling out the vintage where the grapes of wrath are stored. . . ." The words are also the title of John Steinbeck's novel (1938) and the movie made from it (1939). The term *wrath of grapes* is a recent humorous phrase for a hangover.

the grapevine. Some 15 years after Samuel Morse transmitted his famous "what hath God wrought" message, a long telegraph line was strung from Virginia City to

Placerville, California, so crudely strung, it's said, that people jokingly compared the line with a sagging grapevine. I can find no record of this, but, in any case, grapevines were associated with telegraph lines some-where along the line, for by the time of the Civil War a report *by grapevine telegraph* was common slang for a rumor. The idea behind the expression is probably not rumors sent over real telegraph lines, but the telegraphic speed with which rumormongers can transmit canards with their own rude mouth-to-mouth telegraph system.

graveyard stew. During the Great Depression we ate toasted bread and milk, sweetened with a lot of sugar when no one was looking, for too many meals. There were complaints about this *graveyard stew* or *soup*—so named because it was often fed to old people with no teeth or because a steady diet of it might send you to the grave—but it doesn't seem that bad anymore.

gravy. While Italian pasta sauce is often called *red sauce* or simply *sauce* by Italian-Americans, most call the tomato and meat sauce *gravy*. Variants are *spaghetti gravy* and *Sunday gravy*.

gravy train. In the 1920s, railroad men invented the expression to *ride the gravy train* to describe a run on which there was good pay and little work. The words were quickly adopted into general speech, meaning to have an easy job that pays well, or, more commonly, to be prosperous. *Gravy,* however, had been slang for easy money since the early 1900s.

greengage plum. Greengage plums are actually yellow with a tinge of green. The renowned plum, which has two eponymous names, was brought from Italy to France about 1500, where it was named and is still called the Reine-Claude, after Claudia, *la bonne reine,* queen to Francis I from their marriage in 1514 until his death. In about 1725 Sir William Gage, an amateur botanist, imported a number of plum trees from a monastery in France, all of which were labeled except the Reine-Claude. A gardener at Hengrave Hall in Suffolk named the unknown variety Green Gage in honor of his employer and the Reine-Claude has been the greengage in England ever since. The blue and purple gage were developed from their illustrious ancestor on the fertile grounds of Gage's estate, probably much to the delight of his eight children.

grist for the mill. One might think that this 17th-century proverbial saying would be little used today, when many people don't even know that *grist* refers to grain ground to make flour. But *grist for the mill* is commonly heard to denote anything profitable or useful, material that a person can change into something valuable.

grog. Mount Vernon was named after Vice Admiral Sir Edward Vernon by George Washington's half-brother Laurence, who served under "Old Grog" when he led six little ships to the West Indies and captured heavily fortified Portobello during the WAR OF JENKINS' EAR (1739). This action made Vernon England's hero of the hour, Parliament voting him formal thanks and street pageants being held on his birthday to celebrate his humbling of the Spaniards. But the arrogant former war hawk MP never won popularity with his men. Old Grog had been nicknamed for the impressive grogram cloak he wore on deck in all kinds of weather, the coarse taffeta material symbolizing his tough and irascible nature. Then, in August 1740, the stern disciplinarian issued an order that made his name a malediction. In order to curb drunken brawling aboard ships in his command, and to save money, he declared that all rum rations would henceforth be diluted with water. Incensed old sea dogs cursed Vernon roundly, for half a pint of rum mixed with a quart of water seemed weak stuff indeed to any-one on a raw rum liquid diet. Furthermore, the rationed bilge was divided into two issues, served six hours apart. His men soon defiantly dubbed the adulterated rum Grog, using the nickname they had bestowed upon the admiral. Vernon's order served its purpose and "three water rum" became the official ration for all enlisted personnel in the Royal Navy, but *grog* quickly took on the wider meaning of any cheap, diluted drink. *See* BOOZE.

gumbo filé. William Read, in *Louisiana-French Cooking* (1931), explains the origins of this term: "Gumbo [is now] applied to other kinds of gumbo thickened with a powder prepared from sassafrass leaves. This powder goes by the name of *filé*, the past participle of French *filer*, 'to twist'; hence *gumbo filé* signifies properly, 'ropy or stringy gumbo.'"

H

Häagen-Dazs. A rich U.S. ice-cream brand created in 1961. The brand name was coined by Reuben Mattus to create an aura of old-world traditions. According to the *New York Times* (December 1, 2006), they "fabricated the foreign-sounding Danish name . . . putting an umlaut over the first 'a' in Häagen, even though no umlaut is used in Danish."

hair in the butter. A very delicate or sensitive situation. This Americanism dating from the early 20th century refers to the difficulty of removing a single hair from a piece of butter. Wrote Molly Ivins in *Molly Ivins Can't Say That, Can She?* (1991): "The Great Iranian Arms Caper is not only hair in the butter, I'd say someone's thrown a skunk in the church house as well."

halibut. Five hundred years ago every flatfish from the flounder to the skate was called a butt, even the largest of the flounders, *Hippoglossus hippoglossus.* The most esteemed was *Hippoglossus,* which was only eaten on Church holy days and became known as the holy butt. This fish is no longer reserved for holy days, of course, but it is still known as the halibut, or "holy flounder."

hamburger. Most authorities say that the hamburger first appeared in the U.S. in 1884 under the name of *Hamburg steak,* after the place of its origin, Hamburg, Germany. But the town of Hamburg, New York persistently claims that America's favorite quick food was invented there in the summer of 1885 and named for the burger's birthplace. According to this tale, its inventors were Charles and Frank Menches from Ohio, vendors who ran out of pork at their concession at the Erie County Fair. Since the first recorded use of *hamburger* seems to have been in 1902, according to the *O.E.D.*, Hamburg, New York could be the source. *White Castles, McDonalds* and *Wimpeyburgers* (for the Popeye comic-strip character who ate prodigious amounts of them) are synonyms for hamburgers. *See* FRANKFURTER.

hasty pudding. John Bartlett in his *Dictionary of Americanisms* (1850) defines this as "Indian meal stirred into boiling water until it becomes a thick batter or pudding . . . eaten with milk, butter, and sugar or molasses." It is mentioned in a verse of the Revolutionary War song *Yankee Doodle:* "Father and I went down to camp,/ Along wi' Captain Goodin,/ And there we see the men and boys,/ As thick as hasty puddin'." But its most famous mention is in Joel Barlow's mock-epic *The Hasty Pudding* (1793), which the poet wrote in a Savoyard inn in France when he was served a dish of boiled Indian meal that reminded him of Connecticut. Part of it goes:

Thy name is Hasty Pudding! thus our sires
Were wont to greet thee fuming from their fires;
And while they argued in thy just defence,
With logic clear they thus explain'd the sense:
"In *haste* the boiling caldron o'er the blaze
Receives and cooks the ready-powder'd maize;

In *haste* 'tis serv'd; and then in equal *haste,*
With cooling milk, we make the sweet repast."
Such is thy name, significant and clear,
A name, a sound to every Yankee dear.

have other fish to fry. To be busy, usually with something important, so that one can't do anything else at the moment. The old American phrase is still heard today, often with variations, as in this example from the television series *The West Wing* (7/25/01): "I've got a bigger fish to fry."

he hath slept in a bed of saffron. This old Latin expression refers to the supposed exhilarating effects of saffron, meaning "he has a very light heart." As an old poem puts it:

With genial joy to warm his soul,
Helen mixed saffron in the bowl.

One of the most expensive spices, saffron is made from the dried stigmas of crocuses.

hero sandwich; poor boy. New York City's Italian hero sandwiches, the term first recorded in the 1920s, are named for their heroic size, not for Charles Lindbergh or any specific hero of the Roaring Twenties. Hero sandwiches are surely among the most numerous-named things in English. Synonyms include such terms as *hoagies* (in Philadelphia), *submarines* or *subs* (in Pittsburgh and elsewhere), *torpedos* (LosAngeles), *wedgies* (Rhode Island), *wedges* (New York State), *bombers* (New York State), *Garibaldis* (Wisconsin), *Cuban sandwiches* (Miami), *Italian sandwiches* (Maine), *Italians* (Midwest), *grinders* (New England), *spuckies* (pronounced "spookies"; Boston), *rockets* (New York State), *zeps* or *zeppelins* (several states), and *poor boys* (New Orleans), though this last one is made with French instead of Italian bread and can feature oysters. *Blimpie* is a trade name for a similar sandwich, and *Dagwood* refers to any huge sandwich—after "Blondie" comic strip character Dagwood Bumstead's midnight snack creations. That's 20 in all—and there must be more!

hell's kitchen. As that part of hell where the fires are hottest, hell's kitchen would be unpleasant indeed, which is why it came to mean any very unpleasant, disreputable place. The expression is first recorded in Davy Crockett's *An Account of Col. Crockett's Tour to the North and Down East* (1834). By 1879 it was being used as a name for an infamous district on New York City's West Side, which Mitford Mathews tells us was "once regarded as the home of thieves and gunmen." The Stovepipe was part of it, and nearby were the tenements of Poverty Gap.

high on (off) the hog. Well aware that the best cuts of meat on a hog—the hams, pork chops, bacon, tenderloin, and spare ribs—are high up on a hog's sides, American southerners used the expression *eating high on the hog,* "good eating," as opposed to *eating low on the hog*—eating the pig's feet, knuckles, jowls, and sow belly, well known today as "soul food." By extension, *living high on (or off) the hog* came to mean living prosperously.

high tea. Americans are often curious about the meaning of the British expression *high tea,* having no real equivalent for the phrase. High tea is simply a light evening meal, often served at about six o'clock in place of supper, that includes cooked dishes as well as tea, scones, etc.

hobo egg. An egg made by cutting a round center out of a piece of bread, putting the bread in a hot greased pan, dropping the egg into the center without breaking the yolk, and frying the whole until done (sometimes turning it over). Called a "hobo egg" because in the Great Depression era hoboes on the road were said to make it over their fires; called an "Alabama egg" for no reason I've been able to find. Years ago I thought I invented the dish as dinner for my kids, who called it "an egg in the hole in the bread." Actually, I did invent it, but others did, too. I can only add that it is as delicious as the egg sandwiches

Ernest Hemingway describes in his short story "The Battler." Also called gas house eggs.

hock. *Hock,* for any white Rhine wine, is simply an abbreviation of *Hockamore,* which is what the English called *Hochheimer,* a fine white wine made in Hochheim on the River Main in Germany. In commerce the name *hock* became extended to all white Rhine wines, fine or not.

hoecake. It seems unlikely that the cakes of coarse cornmeal called *hoecakes* are so named because they were baked on hoes, for the hoe was a valuable tool on the frontier and baking bread on one would damage and eventually destroy it. More likely the cake takes its name from the Indian *nokehick,* for "coarse cornmeal," which the earliest settlers pronounced *nocake.* These settlers called the cake baked from this meal *nocake,* too, but the name changed to *hoecake* over the years, perhaps because this was close in sound to *nocake* and people thought that *nocake* couldn't possibly be the name for a cake that did exist! All this aside, however, the Japanese *sukiyaki* does mean "shovel-broil," the dish made by Japanese peasants on their shovels.

honeydew melon. *Honeydew* is a popular shortening of "honeydew melon" *(Cucumis Melo inodorus),* a variety developed around 1915 and so named because of its sweetness. Honeydew can also either be the

sweet material that exudes from the leaves of certain plants in hot weather or a sugary material secreted by aphids and other insects. In either case, it gets its name from its sweetness coupled with its dewlike appearance. Spenser wrote of it in

The Faerie Queene:

> Some framed faire lookes, glancing like evening lights,
>
> Others sweet words, dropping like honey dew.

horse potatoes. Said to be "an old word" for yams, much to the surprise of many.

horseradish. There is apparently no truth to old tales that the fiery horseradish *(Armoracia lapathifolia)* is so named because it was once used to cure horses of colds, or because it made a good seasoning for horse meat. *Horse* is used as an adjective before a number of plants to indicate a large, strong, or coarse kind. Others include the horse-cucumber, horse mint, and horseplum. The horse radish is of course hotter, and has a much larger root and leaves than the ordinary radish. However, many plants are named after the horse because they were used to feed or train horses or because they resemble the animal. The horse bean is used as horse feed; horse-bane was supposed to cause palsy in horses; the horse-eye bean was thought to resemble a horse's eye; and the pods of horse-vetch are shaped like horseshoes. The horse chestnut, Gerard says in his famous *Herbal* (1597), bears its name because "people of the East countries do with the fruit thereof cure their horses of the cough . . . and such like diseases." But the horse chestnut is big, too, and when a slip is cut off the tree "obliquely close to the joint, it presents a miniature of a horse's hock and foot, shoe and nails." Incidentally, Samuel Pepys in his *Diary* mentions a *horseradish ale,* ale flavored with horse radish, which must have been hot indeed.

hot cross bun. A sweet bun filled with raisins and marked on the top with a white cross of frosting. Such Lenten buns date back to 16th-century England.

hot dog. According to concessionaire Harry Stevens, who first served grilled franks on a split roll in about 1900, the franks were dubbed hot dogs by that prolific word inventor sports cartoonist T. A. Dorgan after he sampled them. "TAD" possibly had in mind the fact that many people believed frankfurters were made from dog meat at the time, and no doubt heard Stevens' vendors crying out "Get your red hots!" on cold days. Dorgan even drew the hot dog as a dachshund on a roll, leading the indignant Coney Island Chamber of Commerce to ban the use of the term *hot dog* by concessionaires there (they could be called only *Coney Islands, red hots* and *frankfurters). Hot dog!* became an ejaculation of approval by 1906, one that is still heard occasionally; *hot diggity dog!* was invented during the Roaring Twenties. Dorgan at least popularized the term *hot dog,* which may have been around since the late 1880s. *See* FRANKFURTER. In fact, *hot dog* for a frankfurter is recorded in the college newspaper *The Yale Record* in 1895 in a humorous poem about someone who "bites the dog" when it's placed inside a bun.

hot potato. *Hot potato* can mean a "delicate situation," something to be handled with great care. It is said to derive from the phrase *drop someone* (or *something) like a hot potato* and was first recorded in 1950. Over 70 years older, however, is *hot potato* for an energetic person or for a sexy woman, the last sometimes called a *hot patootie,* which was apparently an American invention during World War I.

hotto dogu. The Japa nese borrowing and alteration of the English term *hot dog*. A hamburger is a *hambaga* in Japan, a Coke is a *koka-cora*.

How do you like them apples? An American expression that means "what do you think of that?" *How do you like them apples?* was first recorded in 1941 and is still heard; "*How do you like them grapes?* came on the scene 15 years earlier and may be obsolete today.

Hubbard squash. The tasty squash was bred and first grown over a century ago by Mrs. Elyabeth Hubbard, a Massachussetts gardener. Soon after, it was named in her honor.

huckleberry. The first American settlers noticed the wild huckleberry, comparing it with the English bilberry, and first calling it a *hurtleberry* or *hirtleberry,* from which its present name derives. Huckleberries were so little, plentiful, and common a fruit that a *huckleberry* became early 19th-century slang for a small amount or a person of no consequence, both of these expressions probably inspiring Mark Twain to name his hero Huckleberry Finn. The berry was also used in the colloquial phrase *as thick as huckleberries,* very thick, and *to get the huckleberry,* to be laughed at or ridiculed, a predecessor of sorts of the raspberry (razz), or Bronx Cheer. *To be a huckleberry to someone's persimmon* meant, in 19th-century frontier vernacular, to be nothing in comparison with someone else. Huckleberries, which are not a true berry but a drupe fruit, belong to the *Gaylussacia* genus, which was so named in honor of French chemist Joseph-Louis Gay-Lussac (1778–1850). *See also* BRONX; HOLY COW!

ice wine. According to the *New York Times*, "ice wine is made by pressing grapes that are left on the vine and plucked at the first significant freeze." British Columbia is the best-known area for ice wine.

Idaho baked potato. Very few potatoes are named and known for their place of origin. First known as the Early Rose potato, a variety discovered by the great horticulturist Luther Burbank in his New England garden in 1872, this famed versatile tuber went through some 40 years of breeding before it became known as the Idaho. Strangely enough, this well-known name was made famous by a New York department store "taster." William Titon, better known as Titon the Taster, worked 60 years for Macy's and was the store's final authority on all groceries, wines, and liquors. Among other accomplishments, Titon discovered the Idaho potato in 1926 while buying apples for Macy's and promoted it until the spud's name became synonymous with baked potato, for which Idaho's governor wrote a letter of thanks to the store.

if you peel that onion a little farther. An American expression, its exact origin unknown, meaning "as you examine something a little closer" it begins to take on a new appearance or meaning, as in. "On its surface the tax bill seems to help the poor, but if you peel that onion a little farther, you begin to find that's not the case at all." An onion, of course, has many layers.

"I'll have a steak and the man on the left." Spoken by actress Jayne Mansfield when she first sighted muscleman and Mr. Universe

Mickey Hargitay in a line of body-builders at the Latin Quarter night club. She later married him.

in a pickle. To be in a state of confusion, disorder. The phrase goes at least back to Shakespeare, who writes in *The Tempest* (1611): "I have bin in such a pickle since I saw you last . . ."

in a pretty pickle. *In de pikel zitten*, a Dutch phrase going back at least four centuries, literally means to sit in the salt solution used for preserving pickles. This saying apparently suggested the expression to be in a *pretty pickle*, an uncomfortable or sorry plight—like someone sitting in such a bath. Our word *pickle* comes from the Dutch. A sour pickle is perhaps the last thing anyone would expect to be named after a man, but at least one source claims that the word *pickle* derives from the name of William Beukel or Bukelz, a 14th-century Dutchman who supposedly first pickled fish, inventing the process by which we shrink and sour cucumbers. This pickled-herring theory may be a RED HERRING, however. All the big dictionaries follow the *O.E.D.*'s lead in tracing pickle to the Medieval Dutch word *pekel*, whose origin is ultimately unknown.

Indian bread. Pioneers called the strip of fatty meat extending from the shoulder along the backbone of the buffalo Indian bread because the Indians favored it. As one writer put it: "When scalded in hot grease to seal it, then smoked, it became a 'tit-bit' the buffalo hunter used as bread. When eaten with lean or dried meat it made an excellent sandwich."

I say it's spinach and I say the hell with it. E. B. White wrote the caption that became this catchphrase, for a 1928 Carl Rose cartoon in the *New Yorker* showing a spoiled little girl who rejects her mother's offer of broccoli with these words—which have come to mean, "When I'm indulging my prejudices I don't want to be confused with facts." The phrase's abbreviated form, *spinach*, however, means the same as boloney, malarkey, bull, etc.

it's the berries. The best, the remarkable. An old U.S. expression perhaps inspired by the colorful fruits.

J

java. *Java,* for "coffee," originated as slang among American tramps in the late 19th century. It is obviously an allusion to the coffee-producing island.

Jell-O. The trademark name of this dessert, made of gelatin, sugar, and fruit flavoring, was coined by Mary Wait, the wife of its inventor, cough medicine maker Pearl B. Wait of LeRoy, New York, in 1897. By 1929, Jell-O and Postum cereal were the nucleus of the huge General Foods Corporation.

jelly. Jellies were originally frozen desserts, this reflected by the Latin word *gelata,* meaning "frozen," that is the ancestor of our *jelly,* which is first recorded in 1393. The Romans made their jellies by boiling animal bones. After cooking they set the liquid in a cool place where it solidified, the process suggesting freezing to them.

jerky. *Jerky,* first recorded in 1850, is dried and smoked strips of dried beef. Much used by travelers in the West, *jerky* is simply the Anglicization of the Spanish *charqui* for dried meat, and the Spanish word was often used instead of *jerky. Charqui,* in turn, comes from the Incan *echarqui* for dried meat. *See* BILTONG.

johnnycake. "New England corn pone" someone has dubbed this flat corn bread once cooked on a board over an open fire. Most scholars agree that no cook named Johnny had a hand in inventing the bread. *Johnnycake* is usually traced to *Shawnee cakes* made by the Shawnee Indians, who by Colonial times were long familiar with corn and its many uses in cooking. Not everyone agrees, though, and one popular theory holds that *johnnycake* is a corruption of *journey-cake,* which is what early travelers called the long-lasting corn breads that they carried in their saddlebags. However, *johnnycake* is recorded before *journeycake* in the form of *jonikin*, "thin, waferlike sheets, toasted on a board . . . eaten at breakfast with butter"; *jonikin* is still used for griddle cakes on the eastern shore of Mary land. The word apparently progressed from *Shawnee cake to jonnikin* and *johnnycake*, and then to *journeycake*. Probably when people no longer needed to carry the cakes on journeys, johnnycake became popular again.

Jonathan apple. The Jonathan apple, named after Jonathan Hasbrouck, an American judge who died in 1846, is fifth in order of commercial importance in America. It is a late fall-ripening apple, bright red and often yellow-striped, its round fruit mildly acid and the trees bearing it very prolific. The Jonathan, grown mainly in the Northwest, is but one of numerous apple varieties commending their growers or other notables. The Gravenstein, Grimes Golden, Macoun, and Stayman are only a few others that come to mind.

the juice ain't worth the squeeze. The juice here is orange juice, not liquor, and the saying means it's not worth doing, the effort isn't worth the result. Reported by a Maryland correspondent.

K

kaffeeklatsch. This expression is used, mainly among housewives, as a synonym for the more popular "coffee break." *Klatsch* is German for "a good gossip or gabfest," one held over *kaffee,* or "coffee."

kale. *Kale* is 20th-century American slang for money, as well as a vegetable. The word derives from the Middle English *cale,* a variant of *cole,* for "cabbage." American settlers called this primitive member of the cabbage family *colewarts.*

kedgeree. There's an interesting story behind this delicious dish of rice, fish, milk, and eggs. Originally, this was an Armenian dish called *kidgeri.* Americans not only changed the spelling to *kedgeree,* but substituted eggs for the eggplant that the Armenian recipe calls for.

keep your beard out of my soup. Heard in conversation. Might be a joke, or could be an old expression meaning "mind your own business."

ketchup. Is it *ketchup, catsup, catchup,* or *kitchup?* Since the word derives from the Chinese Amoy dialect *ketsiap,* "pickled fish-brine or sauce," which became the Malay *kechap,* the first spelling is perhaps the best. The original condiment that Dutch traders imported from the Orient appears to have been either a fish sauce similar to the Roman garum or a sauce made from special mushrooms salted for preservation. Englishmen added a "t" to the Malay word, changed the "a" to "u" and began making ketchup themselves, using ingredients like mushrooms, walnuts, cucumbers, and oysters. It wasn't until American seamen added tomatoes from Mexico or the Spanish West Indies to the condiment that tomato ketchup was born. But the spelling and pronunciation "catsup" have strong literary precedents, as witness Dean Swift's: "And for our home-bred British cheer,/ Botargo [fish roe relish], catsup and cabiar [caviar]." (1730). *Catchup* has an earlier citation (1690) than either of the other spellings, predating *ketchup* by some 20 years. *Ketjap,* the Dutch word for the sauce, and *kitchup* have also been used in English. Anyway, a red tide of half a billion bottles of ketchup, catsup, catchup, or kitchup is slopped on everything from Big Macs to vanilla ice cream(!) in America each year.

key lime pie. Named for the tart limes of the Florida Keys, this delicious pie has been part of the Conch cuisine there for well over a century.

kidney bean. The haricot bean takes its name from the French *haricot,* which derived from the Nahuatl Indian *ayacotl* for the bean; it is better known as the *kidney bean* for its shape, resembling a kidney.

kimchee. Korea's traditional kimchee is a very spicy fermented mixture of cabbage, onions, and often fish, highly seasoned with horse radish, garlic, ginger, and red pepper. There are several kinds, the most celebrated being kakutaki kimchee. The dish is often prepared in November and buried in the ground in large earthen jars to preserve it throughout the cold months. South Korean troops fighting in Vietnam had to be supplied with kimchee to bolster their morale, for a Korean meal without it is virtually unthinkable—there is even a Korean proverb saying, "We can live a whole year without meat, but without kimchee we can hardly live a week." Many foreigners, however, find that kimchee burns their palates and complain that it has a strong, unpleasant odor.

Kirby pickle. The Kirby pickle familiar to gardeners is a name applied generally to all pickling cucumbers and definitely is named in honor of a man. It bears the name of the developer of a once-popular pickling cucumber called the *Kirby*—Norvel E. Kirby of Philadelphia's I. N. Simon & Son seed company, now out of business. Simon introduced the Kirby in 1920 and it remained popular until the mid-1930s, when more diseaseresistant types replaced it. Its name remained, however, as a designation for all pickling cucumbers.

knish. A widely popular dish from Jewish cookery, consisting of dough stuffed with potato, cheese, or meat, etc., and baked or fried. The Yiddish word probably comes from the Ukrainian or Polish *knysh,* which, in turn, is of Turkish origin. Leo Rosten in *The Joys of Yiddish* (1968) also gives *knish* as a "vulgarism" for the vagina, and the American poet A.D. Fiske used "Anne Knish" as a pseudonym in *Spectra* (1916), a poetry collection he wrote with Harold Witter Bynner spoofing poetry of the day.

know one's onions. Onions aren't widely known by variety, though the Vidalia and Hawaiian varieties are among several that are well known. Therefore, to speak of someone "who knows his apples," a later variant on the above phrase, would be more appropriate, as there are hundreds of apple varieties. *Know one's onions* was first recorded in 1922 and means to be astute in one's field. An old joke has the esteemed lexicographer C. T. Onions, a longtime editor of the *Oxford English Dictionary,* as the eponym behind the phrase.

kumquat. The Chinese dialect *gamgwat,* "gold citrus fruit," is the origin of the name of this shrub of the genus *Fortunella,* which yields golden citrus fruits, with sweet rinds and an acid pulp, that are used chiefly for preserves.

L

leave in the soup. To leave someone in the lurch or in trouble. The expression is an Americanism first recorded in 1889 in connection with some South Dakota con man who skipped town with a lot of money, leaving many investors in trouble.

lemon. Lemons were probably initially grown in the Middle East, for *lemon* is first recorded as the Persian and Arabic word *limun*, which became the Old French *limon*. Limon passed into English when the French exported the fruit to England, and by the mid-17th century the fruit was being called the lemon there. *Lemon*, meaning something defective or inferior, derives from the sour taste of a lemon and is apparently an Americanism dating back to the turn of the century, as is *lemonade* (a drink the British call "lemon squash"). *See* ZEST. Slot machines with pictures of lemons may have suggested the term *lemon* for anything of inferior quality. One lemon on a machine and the slot machine player loses, which would not endear lemons to any player. The slot machine was invented at the end of the 19th century, just a few years before *lemon* was being used in this sense.

lemonade. As mentioned briefly above, *lemonade* is an Americanism for a drink made of lemon juice, water, and sugar, always served cold, usually with ice. To the British, Australians, and New Zealanders, however, *lemonade* means "clear soda pop," often with a lemon flavor, such as the trademarked Sprite or 7-Up.

lentil; lens. Lentils are the beans that made the mess of pottage that the Bible implies Esau traded his brother for (though Scripture nowhere mentions the phrase "a mess of pottage"); they take their name from the Latin word for the bean, which also gives us the word *lens,* a double convex lens resembling a lentil bean in shape.

lemon sole. Sour lemons have nothing to do with *lemon sole,* except that lemon juice might be squeezed on the fish before eating. The term is an established redundancy; when we say *lemon sole* we are saying "sole sole," for the *lemon* part is a corruption of the French *limande,* for "sole." The sole was so named because its shape was thought to resemble the sole of the foot.

Let them eat cake. Marie Antoinette may have said this in referring to the Paris proletariat after they pleaded for bread in 1770, but she did not invent the famous retort. Rousseau's *Confessions,* written two or three years before the remark is attributed to her, told of a "great princess" who said the same thing to her peasants at least 15 years before Marie Antoinette was born. Some claim that the thoughtless remark was circulated to discredit Marie, while others say she repeated it herself, and she was certainly capable of such a "little joke." The French phrase is *Qu'ils mangent de la brioche* and may mean "they" should eat the outer crust (*brioche*) of the bread, the "stale" part as opposed to the soft inside part.

lettuce. *Lettuce* probably takes its name from a form of the Latin *lactuca,* "milky juice." The Roman gourmet Apicius watered the lettuce in his garden with mead every evening so that it would taste like "green cheese cakes" when he picked it mornings.

life is just a bowl of cherries. Attempts have been made to link this expression with a much older one, *life is but a cherry-fair.* However, the older phrase, from the early 17th century, means life is all too short and fleeting, as short as the annual English fairs held in orchards where cherries were sold each spring. Evanescence is not the spirit of *life is just a bowl of cherries*—which means life is joyous, wonderful, and which seems to have originally been the title of a popular song of the late 19th century.

like the curate's egg. Something satisfactory in some ways but not in others: "The play was rather like the curate's egg." The expression originated with a story in the British magazine *Punch* (November 9, 1895) in which a timid curate had been served a bad egg while dining at the home of an important parishioner. He is asked how the egg tastes and, not wishing to offend his host, says that parts of it are excellent.

like trying to nail Jell-O to a tree. Theodore Roosevelt seems to have invented the idea behind this meta phor, if not the exact words, in a July 2, 1915, letter to William Roscoe Thayer, in which he described the difficulty of negotiating with Colombia regarding the Panama Canal. His exact words were: "You could no more make an agreement with them than you could nail currant jelly to a wall—and the failure to nail currant jelly to a wall is not due to the nail; it is due to the currant jelly."

lima beans. Named for Lima, Peru by early European explorers who found them there, tender lima beans are often called butter beans in the U.S. The succotash made from them (and corn) derives from the Narraganset Indian *msquatash*, literally "fragments." The lima bean's botanical name *Phaseolus* is said to derive from the resemblance between the bean's pod and a special type of ship that originated at Phaselis, a town in Pamphylia.

limburger; Limburger cheese. Limburger cheese was introduced to America by German immigrants in the 19th century and was soon well known for its pungent smell. The soft cheese takes its name from the Limburg province of Belgium (not Holland) where it is made. Its strong smell and flavor long ago made Limburger cheese the butt of many comedians' and cartoonists'

jokes. And since the cheese from Belgium's Limburg province was popularly thought to come from Germany, *Limburger* also became a derogatory term for a German during World War I.

lime; limey. Limes have been cultivated for thousands of years and take their name ultimately from the Persian *liman* for the fruit. As far back as 1795, lime juice was issued in the British navy as an antisorbutic, to protect against scurvy. After about 50 years, Americans and Australians began calling English ships and sailors "lime-juicers," and later "limeys." The term "limey" was eventually applied to all Englishmen, and today the designation and the story behind it are widely known. Originally a contemptuous term and an international slur, *limey* is now considered a rather affectionate designation.

lobster. Lobsters are, in fact, a kind of bug. The word lobster itself is a melding of two foreign words: the Latin *locasta*, meaning "locust," and the Anglo-Saxon *lappe*, which means "spider." "Real" lobster is not the freshwater lobster that the French call *écrevisse*, or crawfish, the small Europe an crustacean with no claws; or even the warm-water spiny lobster from which lobster tails are obtained and labeled *langosta* or *langouste* in some restaurants. The true lobsters number among their ranks only *Homarus* *americanus,* often called Maine, or North Atlantic, lobsters; the smaller blue lobster of Europe, *H. vulgaris; Nephrops norvegicus,* the orange Norwegian lobster, variously called lady lobster, scampi, or prawn; and *H. capensis.*

lobster à l'américaine. *Homard à l'américaine,* as the French call it, is uncooked lobster meat sautéed in oil and served with a rich tomato and white wine sauce. It may have been invented by the chef M. Reculet during the siege of Paris (1870–71) and named in honor of some customer from across the Atlantic. A second explanation holds that the dish originated in Brittany's Armorique, and that its present name is simply a misspelling of *homard à l'armoriquaine.*

lobster Newburg. The most famous of lobster dishes, lobster Newburg, should have blazoned the name of Benjamin J. Wenberg (1835–85), a late 19th-century shipping magnate, across the pages of menus everywhere, but gastronomical lore has it that he was foolish enough to displease the great restaurateur Lorenzo Delmonico. It's said that Wenberg discovered the dish in South America and described it glowingly to Delmonico's owner. Lorenzo, instructing his chef to prepare the shelled lobster in its rich sauce of sherry, thick cream, and egg yolks, served the dish to his wealthy patron and named it *lobster Wenberg* in his honor. It remained thus on Delmonico's menu for almost a month, until one evening when Wenberg got drunk, started a fight in the posh restaurant's dining room and was evicted. Soon after, the dish appeared on an enraged Lorenzo's menu as *lobster Newburg,* probably in honor of the city on the Hudson.

lobster shift. *Lobster shift,* for the newspaper shift commencing at four in the morning, is said to have originated at the defunct *New York Journal-American* early in this century. The newspaper's plant was near the East Side docks and workers on this shift came to work at about the same time lobstermen were putting out to sea in their boats.

lobster Thermidor. Creamy lobster Thermidor may have been invented by a French chef in honor of Napoleon. But some culinary experts contend that this classic fare was named for Victorian Sardou's play *Thermidor* and first served to the public on the evening of January 24, 1874, at the once famous Chez Maire restaurant. According to this account, the controversial drama closed after one per for mance, but the toothsome dish remained a long-running hit.

lollipop. Is the lollipop named after a race horse? The story goes that in the early 1900s one George Smith, a Connecticut candy manufacturer, "put together the candy and the stick" and named it in honor of Lolly Pop, the era's most famous race-horse, the name "lollipop" then becoming an exclusive trade name used by the Bradley-Smith company of New Haven. It is true that candy on a stick wasn't known in America before about 1908 and neither was the word lollipop. Smith may have invented the confection (there are no other claimants) and he may even have named his candy on a stick after the horse in question. But the word *lollipop*, for a piece of sucking candy that dissolves easily in the mouth (*not* one, however, that is attached to a stick) was widely used in England as early as the late 18th century. It apparently derives from the English dialect word *lolly*, used in northern England to mean "tongue," plus the word *pop*, in reference to the sound children made when sucking the candy. Somehow the lollipop remained unknown to Americans until the candy on a stick was invented in the early 20th century, but this is not to say that

the race horse Lolly Pop couldn't have been named for the earlier British term.

looks like she swallowed a watermelon seed. A humorous way American mountain folk describe a pregnant woman. The expression dates back to the early 19th Century.

love apples. Why tomatoes were dubbed "love apples" is a matter of some dispute. First cultivated by the Mayans and called the *xtomatl*, the tomato was named the *pomi del peru* and *mala peruviane* when Cortés brought it to Europe from America. That tomatoes hailed from exotic climes and were a scarlet, shapely fruit undoubtedly helped, but the designation *love apple* owes just as much to semantics as sexuality. All Spaniards at the time were called Moors, and one story has it that an Italian gentleman told a visiting Frenchman that the tomatoes he had been served were *Pomi dei Moro* ("Moor's apples"), which to his guest sounded like *pommes d'amour*, or apples of love. However, another version claims that "apples of love" derives in a similar roundabout way from the Italian *pomo d'oro*, "golden apple," and a third tale confides that courtly Sir Walter Raleigh presented a tomato to Queen Elizabeth, coyly advising her that it was "an apple of love." In any case, the tomato quickly gained a reputation as a wicked aphrodisiac, and justly or not, it has held this distinction ever since. "These Apples of Love ... yield very little nourishment to the body and the same naught and corrupt," the English traveler John Gerard wrote in his 16th-century gardening guide. In Germany the tomato's common name is still *Liebesapfel*, or "love apple," and the expression *hot tomato*, for "a sexy woman," is common to many languages.

lox. Although *bagels* and *lox* are a staple of the Jewish cuisine, the dish is not a staple of long standing. Jews were generally introduced to lox in late 19th century New York, and even today lox is not commonly found in Europe or Israel. Lox is so valued in New York that there have been cases of *counterfeit lox* made from other fish (notably *saithe* from Germany) treated with chemicals and food dyes and sold as the real thing. Real lox is a highly salted smoked salmon.

lox; gox. There is, in addition to the illustrious *lox* (from the Scandinavian *lax,* salmon) of *bagel and lox* fame, a word *lox* used in space research terminology. *Lox* here means *liquid oxygen,* the term used in *lox tank, lox unit,* etc., and as a verb meaning to load the tanks of a rocket vehicle with liquid oxygen. This *lox* came into use in the 1960s and is the antonym of *gox, gaseous oxygen.*

M

macaroni. The word *macaroni* comes from the Greek *makar*, meaning "blessed," which shows how highly it was valued even in ancient times. *Macaroni* meant a well-traveled young Englishman of the 18th century, but also an insufferable fop and a delicious pasta.

malted milk. *Malted milk,* used today for the popular soda fountain drink made of malt, milk, ice cream, and syrup, was once a trademark for a baby food. In 1881 James and William Horlick patented a dried extract of wheat, malted barley, and whole milk "For infants, Invalids, the Aged, and Travelers." The investors coined the trademark Malted Milk, which they enjoyed for many years until it was infringed upon and was eventually applied to the ubiquitous fountain drink.

man for breakfast. Lawlessness often went unpunished in the American West and people reading their morning newspapers had their *man for breakfast,* or murder, every day. The expression persisted from the late 19th century well into the 20th century.

mandarin orange. This fruit either takes its name from the orange, flowing robes of Chinese mandarin officials or from the superiority implied in the title "mandarin." The word is first recorded in an 1816 botanical treatise.

mango. The mango is one of the most important of tropical fruits. Mango varieties number in the hundreds. Some of the notable dessert mangoes are the Alphonse of Bombay, the Ferdandin of Goa and the Kimayuddin of South India. The delectable fruit, whose name derives from the Portuguese *manga,* taken from its Malayan name, or from the Chinese *man-guoh,* meaning hair-fruit, is grown in the American South, but these varieties can't be compared to tropical ones in taste. One Indian poet described mangoes as "sealed jars of paradisical honey"; the Buddha was given a grove of them so that he could sit in the shade and meditate; and a Hindu god, Subramanya, renounced the world because he couldn't obtain a mango he desired. The mango isn't a difficult fruit to eat once you get the hang of cutting the pulp away from its large central seed, but it might be better to eat it in a bathtub to avoid the explosion of juice that is common to novices. The nutritious mango tastes something like a peach, but the comparison is wholly inadequate. An attractive bright yellow and red fruit, it hangs like a pendulum from its long stem. A building in Angkor that dates to A.D. 961 bears the following quotation under one of its most beautiful female figures: "Drawn by the flower of its glory to the fruit of the beauty of the mango tree of her body . . . the eye of man could nevermore tear itself away."

many small potatoes and few in a hill. New Englanders, especially Mainers, use this expression for something or somebody of small consequence. It dates back about a century.

maple syrup; maple sugar. "There can't be a remedy better for fortifying the stomach" than maple sugar, a pioneer wrote in 1705. Maple sugar, boiled from maple syrup and the only sugar the first settlers had, has a long history that dates from the time American pioneers learned how to make it from the Indians. The same, of course, applies to maple syrup, another maple-tree product Americans are still familiar with, but there were also maple-derived products like maple water, maple vinegar, maple molasses, maple wax, maple beer, and even maple wine.

margarine. The Latin *margarita,* "pearl," is the ancestor of *margarine,* which, before dyes were commonly added, was a white, pearl-like substance extracted from hog's lard. *Oleomargarine* (from the Latin *oleum,* "oil," plus *margarine*) was coined first, in 1854, by the French chemist Marcellin Berthelot, and shortened to *margarine* in the U.S. by 1873.

marmalade. Though made today of oranges and lemons, the conserve called marmalade takes its name from the Latin *melimelum* or "honey apple," which was some variety of apple grafted on quince stock. The Latin for "honey apple" became the Portuguese word for "quince," and the first marmalades recorded, in the early 16th century, were made of quinces and brought to England from Portugal. But over the centuries there have been plum, cherry, apple, and even date marmalades as well. "Natural marmalade" is the fruit of the marmalade tree *(Lucuma mammosa).*

marrow. *Marrow* is a British term that is sometimes used in America. It means "a long, green squash," and has its origins in the use of *marrow* as the term for the pulp of a fruit, which dates back to at least the 10th century. Squash was often called marrowsquash in 18th-century America.

the marshmallows of the sea. A name sometimes given to ocean scallops because of their shape.

martini. H. L. Mencken traced the martini to 1899 and traces the cocktail's name from the Martini and Rossi firm, maker of a popular vermouth. Others say the drink originated with a now forgotten Italian or Spanish bartender named Martini. The dry martini is made, according to the classic recipe, by drinking a little vermouth, exhaling into the interior of a cocktail glass and filling it with gin—after you drink it, you'll forget that you forgot the olive. Mencken also mentions the *martini sandwich,* a dry martini between two glasses of beer, which he says "is favored by many American linguists." Novelist George V. Higgins called the martini "loud-mouth soup."

matzo. This unleavened bread in the form of large, square corrugated crackers takes its name from the Hebrew-Arabic *massah,* "to touch, handle, squeeze," in reference to making the bread. *Matzo* thus has the same root as "massage."

marzipan. A confection made of almond paste and sugar molded in various forms. One sweet fable tells of a cook of 16th-century Brandenberg, Germany, named Franz Marzip, who is said to have invented marzipan for his physician employer. Other sources say that Oriental rulers had enjoyed the confection for centuries and that the crusaders brought it back to Europe in the shape of a coin of the time called a *marchpane* (which later became *marzipan).* In any case, Lubbeck, Germany is called "the world's marzipan capital" today, famous for its *Holstentors,* cuisine's most celebrated marzipan.

mayonnaise. Port Mahon gave its name to *mayonnaise.* The story is that the duc de Richelieu attacked the Spanish island of Minorca and drove out the British for a while in 1756. But Richelieu was ravenously hungry after the battle. The Frenchman stormed the nearest kitchen ashore, tossed all the food he could find into one pot and blended it all together. This apocryphal tale got back to Paris, where chefs concocted a dressing of blended-together ingredients that they named *Mahonnaise* in honor of Richelieu's victory at Port Mahon.

mean enough to take his wife's egg money. Said of a very stingy man, one so cheap he would steal or forcibly take the pin money a woman had saved by selling eggs, etc.

meat. *Meat* in Middle English meant food in general. The word became confined to the flesh of animals when there was a large increase in flesh eating and *meat* by the 17th century lost its meaning of food in general.

meat and potatoes. Over the years *meat and potatoes* has come to mean "the simple fundamentals" because a meat course and potato course are so often principal parts of a meal. *Meat and drink* means food in general. *See* POTATO.

melba toast; peach melba. Melba toast, according to the traditional story, originated as several pieces of burnt toast served to the Australian opera star Dame Nellie Melba at the Savoy in London. The prima donna had been on a diet, ordered toast, and enjoyed the crisp, crunchy, overtoasted slices that were served to her by mistake. The maitre d' named them in her honor and put melba toast on the menu. Whether the story is true or not, thin crispy melba toast honors Dame Nellie, as does the peach melba, which the French chef Escoffier concocted for her. Nellie Melba was the stage name adapted from the city of Melbourne by Helen Porter Mitchell (1861–1931), who became a Dame of the British Empire in 1918. The world-famous soprano made her debut in *Rigoletto* in Brussels (1887) and went on to star at London's Covent Garden, the Paris Opera, La Scala, and New York's Metropolitan among numerous opera houses. Unlike many opera stars, Nellie Melba did not study singing until she was over 21 years old, although she had previously been trained as a pianist.

melons. There are so many melons that it would be near impossible to treat them here. All melons, however, are nutritious foods, particularly high in vitamins A and C. An old piece of doggerel compares men and melons, with melons decidedly the winner:

> Men are like melons,
> Shall I tell you why?
> To find a good one
> You must one-hundred try.

mighty small potatoes and few to a hill. This old Americanism is heard more often today in its abbreviated form *small potatoes*. Both expressions mean someone or something of little consequence, insignificant, and were first recorded in 1831. A variation is *small potatoes and few in a hill.*

mint. *Mint* derives from the name of the Greek nymph Mint-he, who was transformed into the herb by Proserpine, the jealous wife of Pluto, god of the underworld. Wild mint *(Mentha sativa)* has been chewed since earliest times and is often regarded as an aphrodisiac. Aristotle forbade the chewing of mint by Alexander the Great's soldiers because he felt it aroused them erotically and sapped their desire to fight.

miracle fruit. When chewed together, the berrylike fruits of the African shrub *Synsepalum dulcificum* and *Thaumatococcus daniellii* make sour substances taste sweet. For this reason they are called the "miracle fruit," "miracle berry," "miraculous fruit," and "serendipity berry." Another African shrub, *Dioscoreophyllum cumminsii*, goes by the same names for the same reason.

mocha. The Arabian Red Sea port of Mocha gave its name to the variety of coffee called mocha sometime in the early 15th century, when it was a leading exporter of coffee beans. It was only when chocolate was flavored with mocha coffee centuries later that *mocha* became the word for a chocolate brown color. Today the city of Mocha is in Yemen and is called Mukka.

the Moon is made of green cheese. Often credited to Sir Thomas More and Rabelais, this proverb actually dates back to at least the early 15th century. Even then it was assumed that anyone who believed the moon was made of green cheese, or "cream cheese," as one writer put it, was a complete fool. Originally the expression was *The moone is made of a green cheese.* Green cheese wasn't a cheese green in color, but a new cheese that hadn't aged properly yet and resembled the full moon in shape.

Molotov cocktail. This "cocktail for Molotov" was so named by the Finns while fighting the Russians in 1940. The Russians were dropping bombs on Helsinki at the time, but Russian statesman Vyacheslav Mikhailovich Molotov (1890–1986) claimed that they were only dropping food and drink to their comrades. This equation of food and drink with bombs quickly resulted in the black-humorous term *Molotov breadbasket* for an incendiary bomb and then *Molotov cocktail* for a gasoline-filled bottle with a slow burning wick that is ignited before the crude incendiary is thrown; when the bottle hits the ground it bursts and the ignited gasoline spreads over its target. The weapon had first been used by the Chinese against Japanese tanks in 1937. Molotov was Soviet premier at the time the Finns derisively named the "cocktail" after him. He had only the year before negotiated the infamous Russo- German nonaggression pact, which is sometimes called the Molotov-Ribbentrop pact but is best known as the Pact of Steel. Molotov, a communist from his early youth, changed his name from Skriabin to escape the Czarist police. (*Molotov* comes from *molot*, Russian for "hammer.") He rose quickly in the party hierarchy, serving in many capacities. In 1940 the city of Perm was renamed Molotov in his honor, but the wily diplomat later fell into disfavor, being sharply attacked by Khrushchev at the 22nd Party Congress in 1961, and was expelled from the Communist Party, to which he was readmitted in 1984.

Monterey Jack. A mild American cheddar cheese said to have been named about 1945 after its inventor, David Jack, and Monterey County, California.

Mornay sauce. French Protestant leader Philippe de Mornay (1549–1623) invented *sauce Mornay* for King Henry IV. Made with fish broth, the white sauce is enriched with Parmesan and Gruyere cheese and butter. Popularly known as the Protestant Pope, Mornay was Henry's right-hand man until the king converted to Catholicism and the Seigneur Duplessis-Mornay fell out of favor. After Henry's assassination, Louis XIII finally retired Mornay as governor of Saumur because of his opposition to the government's rapprochement with Catholic Spain. Mornay's spiritual writings and organizing abilities strongly influenced the development of a Protestant party in France.

moscato. Everything is not swell with muscatel. *Moscato*, or *muscatel*, is a rich, sweet wine. According to Bill Bryson's excellent *Mother Tongue* (1990), its name in Italian means "wine with flies in it." *Mosca* means *"fly"* in Italian.

mouth-watering. Cavemen 100,000 years ago surely felt their mouths watering over the smell and sight of meat roasting in their fires, but this expression somehow wasn't recorded until 1555 in English. Soon after, this term for appetizing came to be used figuratively as well as literally.

moveable feast. A church feast that doesn't fall on the same date every year, that isn't "fixed." *A Moveable Feast* (with an "e" in the title) is a 1964 memoir by Ernest Hemingway consisting of sketches of the author and his many friends and acquaintances in Paris, 1921–26.

moxie. The rather bitter, tart, unsweetened flavor of Moxie, a popular New England soft drink, or tonic, as soda pop is often called in the area, has been suggested as the reason it yielded the slang word *moxie,* for "courage, nerve, or guts." Or maybe, Moxie braced up a lot of people, giving them courage. These are only guesses, but the tonic, a favorite since at least 1927, is definitely responsible for *a lot of moxie* and other phrases, which, however, aren't recorded until about 1939. But Moxie was originally made in 1884 as a patent medicine nerve tonic said to cure "brain and nervous exhaustion, loss of manhood, softening of the brain, and mental imbecility." This goes far in explaining *moxie*, "nerve or courage," if earlier uses for the term could be found. In any event, Moxie's Lowell, Massachusetts makers fizzed up their product toward the turn of the century when the government began cracking down on their health claims and Moxie became America's first mass-market soft drink, the company even selling their product in "Moxiemobiles," car-shaped bottles.

mulligan stew. Mulligan stew is made of meat and vegetables—whatever is available or can be begged or stolen. It is an American term, honoring an Irishman whose first name has been lost but who may have made a tasty Irish stew. Mulligan, popular among American tramps, is also called slumgullion, or slum, the term coming into use during the American gold rush when slumgullion was originally the muddy residue remaining after sluicing gravel.

mung bean; bean sprouts. The Asian mung bean takes its name from the Tamil *mungu* meaning the same. These are the beans that are easiest to sprout, taking barely three days, and are used for Chinese *bean sprouts*.

mushroom. When Englishmen in the 15th century tried to pronounce the French word for this succulent fungus, *mousseron,* it came out "muscheron," which over the years became "mushroom," this pronunciation probably to some extent influenced by the common English words *mush* and *room*. All in all, they may have been better off with their native name for the edible fungus: *toad's hat*. "Toad's hat" is no longer heard, but *toadstool* is of course still the name for inedible, poisonous mushrooms. The French word *mousseron,* from which mushroom sprang up, is generally accepted as a derivative of *mousse,* "moss," upon which mushrooms grow. Cities that sprang up rapidly, that seemed to spring up like mushrooms overnight, were called *mushrooms* in England as early as 1787. Within another century the name became a verb meaning to spread out, being first applied to bullets that expand and flatten, then to fires, and then to anything that grows rapidly. The fungus called a *mushroom* takes its name from the Latin *mussirio* meaning the same.

mushroom cloud. This image for the explosion of an atomic bomb was first used by *New York Times* reporter William L. Laurence in reporting the initial test of the bomb on July 16, 1945, near Alamogordo, New Mexico. Laurence called the cloud a "supramundane mushroom:" "At first it was a giant column that soon took the form of a supramundane mushroom. For a fleeting instant it took the form of the Statue of Liberty magnified many times."

mustard. Mustard takes its name from the *must* or "new wine" that was first used in mixing the paste, which is made from various plants of the *Brassica* genus, including, chiefly, *Brassica nigra,* "black mustard," and *Brassica hirta,* "white mustard." Frederick the Great believed mustard did so much for his masculinity that he invented a drink made with powdered mustard, champagne, and coffee. The history of hot mustard as an aphrodisiac is a long one. Rabelais, for example, writes that his lusty Demisemiquaver friars "began their meal with cheese, ending it with mustard and lettuce, as Martial tell us the ancients did. As each received a dishful of mustard after dinner, they made good the old proverb: Mustard after dinner / is good for saint and sinner."

mustard gas. The first gas used in World War I. The oily volatile liquid blistered the skin, damaged the lungs, and often caused blindness or death. Introduced by the Germans in 1915, it was named "mustard gas" after its mustardlike odor and the taste it left on the tongue. It is scientifically called dichlorodiethyl sulfide.

mutton dressed as lamb. An old expression describing old (or middle-aged) people trying to look or dress as if they were younger or richer. The allusion may be to a butcher dressing meat. The words seem to be 18th-century British in origin, like *muttonhood,* which meant "adulthood" a century ago and *lamb,* which meant a "virgin."

N

navel orange. The first navel orange was a "bud-sport" that originated for reasons unknown from the bud of an otherwise normal orange tree in a monastery garden in Bahia, Brazil, from where it was imported into the U.S. in 1870. This sweet, usually seedless orange takes its name from the depression in its rind resembling a human navel, which contains an aborted ovary that appears as a small secondary fruit within the fruit. Many other varieties, however, exhibit this characteristic at times.

new potatoes. Small, often thin-skinned red potatoes, so called because they are often the first of the season. They are also called "salad potatoes," because they are frequently used in potato salad, and "salt potatoes," because they are boiled in salted water. Another interesting potato term, not often heard anymore, is the 19th-century expression *shadow potatoes* for potato chips.

No more free lunch! When he was elected in 1934, New York's reform mayor Fiorello La Guardia invented the slogan "No More Free Lunch!" (No more graft). The words are a translation of the Italian "E finite la cuccagna!" said to have been shouted by the Little Flower while he angrily shook his fist at City Hall.

not by bread alone. This ancient expression, meaning that a person's spirit must be cared for as well as his body, comes from the Bible (Deut. 8:3): "Man doth not live by bread alone, but by every word that proceedeth out of the mouth of the Lord doth man live."

not worth a bean. One of the oldest expressions in English, recorded as early as the 13th century and colloquial since at least 1400. Beans have little commercial value compared to other foods because they are so easy to grow and prolific, even the garden "hill of beans" in the American version of the English expression. The hill in "not worth a hill of beans" was a common term a century ago when the saying was born. It means not an actual hill but a group of bean plants planted close together in a circle. Because most people plant beans in straight rows now and the meaning of hills is unclear to many, the phrase used today is usually not worth a row of beans.

not to know beans. The nationally used not to know beans may initially have been a Boston expression, suggesting that anyone who didn't know how to make baked beans in Boston, "the home of the bean and the cod," would have to be incredibly ignorant.

not to know beef from bulls' foot. A phrase meaning to be exceedingly dumb; also not to know B from bull's foot, not to know bees from bull's foot, and not to know beeswax from bull's foot.

not worth a row (hill) of beans. The meaning behind this phrase is that beans have little value compared with other crops because they are so easy to grow and prolific. *Not worth a bean* is one of the oldest expressions in English, recorded as early as the 13th century and

colloquial since at least 1400. The *hill* in *not worth a hill of beans,* in the American version of the English expression, was a common term a century ago when the saying was born. It means not an actual hill, but a group of bean plants planted close together in a circle. Because most people now plant beans in straight rows and the meaning of hills is unclear to many, the phrase is usually *not worth a row of beans* today.

northern fox grape. A wild grape ranging from New England to Illinois and south to Georgia that is so named because it supposedly "smelleth and tasteth like unto a foxe." It is the source of the Concord and other cultivated grape varieties.

nosh. To nosh is to snack or eat between meals, while a nosh is a snack. A Yiddish contribution to English first recorded in about 1955, *nosh* is ultimately from the German *naschen,* "to eat on the sly."

nut. Due to the round shape of many nuts, *nut* has long been slang for "head," which led to the expression, *he's off his nut* meaning "he's crazy," which in turn gave us *nuts* for "crazy" and *nut house,* meaning "insane asylum." The word *nut* can be used for a sum of money, and figures in many other expressions as well, including *a hard nut to crack* (a tough problem to solve) and *from soup to nuts,* meaning "complete." To give someone a brief summary of something is *to put it in a nutshell* and obviously refers to the small size of a nutshell. The phrase has been with us at least since Pliny reported that the *Iliad* had been copied in so small a handwriting by a contemporary of his that the whole work fit in a walnut shell. This feat has been duplicated several times over the years. Since there are no nuts to be gathered in May, the old children's song with the words, "Here we go gathering nuts in May" seems to make no sense—and indeed, it may have been intended as a nonsense song. But "the nuts" in the phrase has been explained as being "knots" of May, that is, bunches of flowers. In Elizabethan England, Queen Elizabeth herself gathered knots of May in the meadows, one author tells us, and this is a plausible explanation even though there are no recorded quotations supporting the use of *knots* for "flowers," except possibly the English *knot garden* of herbs.

okra. Okra was so valuable in ancient Angola that tribes made "sharp knife" raids into neighbors' fields to steal the vegetable, killing anyone who stood in their way. *Okra* derives ultimately from the Tshi *nkruman.* The Arabs held it to be a rare delicacy fit for weddings and other special occasions, naming it *uehka,* which means "a gift." Okra is sometimes called ladyfingers in England, this name being suggested by the shape of the pods.

old chestnut. English playwright William Dimond's melodrama *The Broken Sword* (1816) is all but forgotten, along with its characters, plot, and dialogue, and the author himself isn't remembered in most guides to literature. Yet Dimond had found immortality of sorts in the expression *an old chestnut,* "a stale joke or story," which probably derives from an incident in his play. *The Broken Sword*'s principal character is crusty old Captain Xavier, who is forever spinning the same yarns about his highly unlikely experiences. He begins to tell the following one to Pablo, another comic character:

> *Captain Xavier:* I entered the woods of Golloway, when suddenly from the thick boughs of a cork tree—
> *Pablo:* A chestnut, Captain, a chestnut!
> *Captain Xavier:* Bah, I tell you it was a cork tree.
> *Pablo:* A chestnut; I guess I ought to know, for haven't I heard you tell this story twenty-seven times?

Fame didn't come immediately. The lines lay at rest in Dimond's play for almost 70 years before American actor William Warren, Jr. repeated them at a stage testimonial dinner in Boston, after hearing another speaker tell a stale joke. Other actors present adopted Warren's *chestnut,* elaborated on it, and it became the timeworn *old chestnut.*

olive. *Wine within, oil without,* was the Roman formula for a happy life, and the oil with which they anointed their bodies was, of course, olive oil. Olives themselves were believed to stimulate drinking by the Romans, whose word *oliva* for the fruit became our *olive.* So interwoven is the olive with history—Noah's biblical olive branch the symbol of peace; some of the ancient olive trees in the Garden of Gethsemane possibly growing there since the time of Christ's betrayal; Athens named for the goddess Athena after she gave the olive to man—that books have been written about the fruit. The olive tree, which has been known to live well over 1,000 years, was simply a staple of life, yielding both food and light (from lamp oil) and grown also for its symbolism of joy, happiness, and peace. Green olives are those picked early; the black ones are picked ripe. Both are very bitter indeed before they are soaked in a lye and salt solution and readied for market.

one foot on a banana peel and the other in the grave. Very old or very ill, on the brink of death, slipping away fast; or not in good health recently, though far from dying. The words are a 20th-century humorous

extension of ONE FOOT IN THE GRAVE.

one man's meat. The complete saying is one man's meat is another's poison; that is, what is good for one person can be bad for another. A slight variation is one man's meat is another man's poison. American humorist E. B. White wrote the One Man's Meat Department for *Harper's* magazine from 1938 to 1943 and also wrote the *New Yorker's* Talk of the Town essay columns.

One Meat Ball. A song written by Hy Zaret, one of the most prolific and successful Tin Pan Alley lyricists. Zaret died on July 30, 2007, at the age of 99. *One Meat Ball* told a story of a poor man in the Great Depression years who had only 15 cents for a meatball. Among the many songs Mr. Zaret wrote were *So Long for Awhile, Unchained Melody, There I Go Again;* and *The Partisan.* At the time of his death he was working on *Love Song for Senior Citizens.*

onion. *Onion* comes from the Latin word *unio,* "oneness" or "union," in reference to the many united layers in an onion; the Romans used the same word for the multilayered pearl; thus our pearl onion would have been a Roman *unio unio.* Onions were fed to the Egyptian laborers who built the great Cheops pyramid, dispensed by Alexander the Great to his troops to promote valor, and praised by General Grant, who once wired the War Department that he would not move his army farther without onions. The onion is believed by some to be an aphrodisiac as well as strength-giving, though as Shakespeare wrote, "Eat no onions or garlic, for we are to utter sweet breath."

orange. The Sanskrit word *narange* became the Latin *aurangia,* "golden apple," from which our *orange* derives. *Portugals* is a name still used for sweet oranges in Greece, Albania, Italy, and the Middle East, for bitter oranges were the only oranges known in Europe until Portuguese ships brought sweet oranges back from India in 1529. Later, in 1645, still-sweeter Chinese oranges reached Lisbon, and they are responsible for the scientific name for the modern sweet orange, *Citrus sinensis* (*sinensis* is Latin for "Chinese"). Sweet oranges were a luxury enjoyed mainly by royalty until the mid 19th century. Thousands of varieties of fruits are named after their developers, and in this regard the orange is no exception. The best-known eponymous orange variety is the *Temple.* Others include the *Murcott Honey* orange, named for Florida grower Charles Murcott Smith, and the *Parson Brown,* which honors Nathan L. Brown, a Florida clergyman. The United States is by far the largest grower of oranges, producing more than 25 billion a year. An orange's

color, incidentally, has nothing to do with its ripeness. Oranges turn orange only as a result of cold weather, which breaks down a membrane protecting their green chlorophyll. This is why summer oranges are often dyed and stamped with the words "color added." Long the traditional decoration for a bride in England, the orange blossom is said to indicate purity because of its whiteness, and fruitfulness because the orange tree is so prolific.

oregano. An aromatic herb also called pot marjoram and joy of the mountain, when gathered wild. Widely used as a cooking seasoning.

other fish to fry. To have other, often more important, things to do. A variation is to have bigger fish to fry. The first recorded use of the expression is in British author John Evelyn's *Memoirs* (1660): "I fear he hath other fish to fry."

our bread is buttered from the same plate. Our interests are the same. An old proverb that seems to have originated at least in the 18th century but isn't used much today.

our cake is dough. This expression, for "miscarried plans and disappointments," goes back before Shakespeare, who used it in *The Taming of the Shrew.* It is first recorded in Thomas Beacon's *Prayers* (1559): "Or else your cake is dough, and all your fat lie in the fire."

oysters Kirkpatrick. Oysters Kirkpatrick was named in honor of James C. Kirkpatrick, manager of San Francisco's Palace Hotel in the late 19th century. The Palace Hotel, born during the gold rush of 1849, destroyed in the earthquake of 1906 and rebuilt to become one of America's greatest eating places, offers the following simple original recipe for the delectable dish: "Open oysters on deep shell, put in oven for about 3 or 4 minutes until oysters shrink. Pour off the liquor, then add small strip of bacon and cover with catsup and place in very hot oven for about 5 to 6 minutes until glazed to a nice golden brown."

P

papaya. The versatile *papaya,* or tree melon, is a staple food in many parts of the world, and its enzyme *papain* aids in the digestion of food, one reason why its leaves are used as a meat tenderizer in some countries and the fruit is the basis for commercial tenderizers. Indians of Central America gorge themselves with *pawpaw* so that they can eat large quantities of food at their feasts without becoming ill. The word *papaya* is a corruption of the Carib Indian *ababai.* In Cuba and some other Spanish-speaking countries the large fruit (it sometimes weighs up to 20 pounds) is called *fruta bomba,* or "bomb fruit." *Papaya* itself has come to be slang for "the female fruit," or breasts, in Cuba, but isn't used in polite conversation.

Parmesan cheese. *Parmesan* is simply English for the Italian word *Parmigiano,* of Parma, and thus the latter word should be the name of the hard, often grated cheese. Parmigiano was once made mostly from milk from the old Italian duchy of Parma.

parsley. "Parsley grows for the wicked, but not for the just," according to an old English proverb. Parsley takes its name ultimately from the Greek *petroselinon* for the herb. This member of the celery family began earning its shady reputation even before the Romans, who wore curly-leaved parsley garlands in their hair not only because they were attractive but because they believed that nibbling on parsley sprigs enabled one to drink more wine without becoming drunk. The Greeks crowned winning athletes with parsley at their Nemean and Isthmian games, and used the herb as a flavoring. The Romans fed it to their horses on the theory that it made them swift. The plant is described by Seneca, who notes that the tempting sorceress Medea gathered parsley and other forbidden herbs by moonlight.

pasta. There are some 500 Italian words describing various types of pasta. *Pasta* is simply Italian for dough and can be anything from cappelletti to ziti. *See* SPAGHETTI.

pasta fazool. There is no such Italian dish—not spelled this way. *Pasta fazool* is the Neapolitan-American pronunciation of *pasta e fagioli,* a soup containing beans (*fagioli*), other vegetables, and little *ditalini* pasta.

pastrami; pistol. Pastrami is a highly seasoned, smoked shoulder cut of beef, its name deriving from the Rumanian *pastrama.* U.S. deli workers may call pastrami pistol ("Pistol-shoot it all the way!") because, as the *New Dictionary of American Slang* humorously suggests, the eater of a hot pastrami sandwich "feels as if shot in the stomach soon after eating it."

PB&J; peanut butter; jelly. PB & J is recent shorthand, written and verbal, for a peanut butter and jelly sandwich. *Peanut butter* itself is first recorded in about 1890 as the health food invention of a St. Louis dentist, while the word *jelly* dates back to the 14th century. *See* PEANUT.

pea. The word *pea* comes indirectly from the Latin *pisum,* "pea"; the early English singular for pea was *pease,* hence the old rhyme "pease-porridge hot, / Pease-porridge cold, / Peaseporridge in the pot, / Nine days old." Quite a mania for peas existed in 17th-century France. Madame de Maintenon, Louis XIV's mistress, called it "both a fashion and a madness," and it was at this time that the celebrated *petits pois à la française* was invented. Incidentally, it was quite proper at the time to lick green peas from their shells after dropping the whole pod in a sauce, so eating peas off a knife isn't so bad after all. Chinese sugar or snow peas, eaten pod and all, are sometimes properly called *mangetout* ("eat all"). *Till the last pea's out of the dish* is a southern Americanism meaning "till the end," or "a long time." Red Barber popular ized the southern expression *tearing up the pea patch* for "going on a rampage" when he broadcast Brooklyn Dodger baseball games from 1945 to 1955, using it often to describe fights on the field between players. Barber came from the South, where the expression is an old one, referring to the prized patch of black-eyed peas, which stray animals sometimes ruined. "English peas" is a term used in the South for green peas to distinguish them from the black-eyed or browneyed varieties. *See* BLACKED-EYED PEAS.

peach. Peaches were the "Persian apples" of the ancient Romans. Their name, *Persicum,* became *pessica* in Late Latin, *pêche* in French, and finally came into English as *peach.* The fruit, luscious to look at, touch, and taste, has described a pretty young girl at least since the ancient Chinese used it as slang for a young bride centuries ago. But the Chinese, and the Arabs, too, also regarded the peach's deep furedged cleft as a symbol of the female genitalia and used *peach* in a number of slang expressions referring to sexual love, such as *sharing the peach,* a euphemism for sodomy. In Europe the French have used their word *pêche* in similar sexual expressions and *a peach house* was once common in English slang as a house of prostitutes. "Venus owns this tree . . . the fruit provokes lust," English herbalist Nicholas Culpeper wrote in 1652 and language reflects that people around the world shared his opinion. The *Elberta peach,* the most widely sold of American peaches, was probably imported from Shanghai in 1850, but more than one source records a story that shows more imagination. According to this tale, Samuel Rumph of Marshallville, Georgia, received peach-tree buddings from a friend in Delaware, planted them, and eventually harvested a good crop. His wife, Elberta, accidentally dropped a few pits from these peaches in her sewing basket and when their grandson wanted to start an orchard 10 years later, she dug them out and asked her husband to plant them. By 1870 trees from the pits were flourishing, and by an accidental cross-pollination a new golden variety resulted, which Rumph named for his spouse. Elbertas, however, aren't considered great eating peaches by those who know their peaches.

peanut; peanut gallery. Peanuts take their name from their resemblance to peas in a pod. They go by numerous descriptive aliases, including *monkey nuts* and *ground peas* or *nuts,* but their most common synonym, *goober,* is a corruption of *nguba,* a name plantation slaves gave to the peanut and one of the few African words still retained in English. Peanuts are used in hundreds of products. Peanut butter, for example, is an easily-digested, high-protein food that nutritionists say provides an adequate survival diet when combined with a citrus fruit like oranges. Four out of five American homes are said to stock a jar of it in the pantry. Americans aren't as partial to peanut butter soup, or to the dish called Young Monkey Stuffed with Peanuts invented by futurist chef Jules Maincave during World War 1. The peanut gallery, usually the cheapest seats in the house, was the gallery, or "second balcony," high up in Gay Nineties theaters, so high up that the crowd seated there were sometimes called the gallery gods. Peanuts were the movie snack of the day and the occupants of these cheap seats often rained peanut shells on performers who displeased them. *See* PB&J.

pea souper; pea soup fog. These terms originated in England toward the end of the 19th century. They describe a dense, yellowish fog or any very thick fog through which a fisherman can barely see the end of his outstretched arm.

Peel me a grape. This humorous request or command stems from an early Mae West movie in which the "Screen's Bad Girl" tells her maid (Louise Beavers) to do same: "Peel me a grape, Beulah." There is a 2002 song "Peel Me A Grape," a favorite of sexy singers.

Peeps. The name of those yellow marshmallow chicks that are almost always found in childrens' Easter baskets. Originally made by the Rodda Candy Co., they have since 1954 been the property of Just Born, Inc., in Bethlehem, Pennsylvania. Some 1.5 billion of them are produced every year, each thickly coated with sugar and costing the consumer 32 calories. Recently they are being made in other colors and shapes besides yellow chicks.

pepper. *Pepper* can be traced back to the Sanskrit *pippali,* for a type of condiment pepper that comes from the dried berries of a climbing shrub. Garden peppers are not related to this shrub, but received the same name when Columbus discovered hot varieties of the garden pepper in the West Indies and wrongly believed they were a new variety of the condiment pepper. *See also* CHILI PEPPER.

persimmon. *See* EATIN' A GREEN 'SIMMON.

pho. A new word, unrecorded in any dictionary, that entered the language with Vietnamese immigrants to the U.S., pho is a noodle soup with beef that is becoming more popular every year. It is said that along Garden Grove Boulevard in Orange County, California, "it is easier to lunch on pho . . . than on a hamburger."

Pickle Factory. A little-known nickname of the CIA, among its members, in the Central Intelligence Agency's early days of the late 1940s and 1950s. The CIA is also called the Company.

pie. Pie is an old English word of obscure origin, first recorded in 1275. Wrote Harriet Beecher Stowe in *Old Town Folks* (1869): "The pie is an English institution, which, planted on American soil, forthwith ran rampant and burst forth into an untold variety of genera and species. Not merely the old traditional mince pie, but a thousand strictly American seedlings

from the main stock, evinced the power of American housewives to adapt old institutions to new uses. Pumpkin pies, cranberry pies, huckleberry pies, peach, pear and plum pies, custard pies, apple pies, Marlborough-pudding pies—pies with top crusts and without—pies adorned with all sorts of fanciful flutings and architectural strips laid across and around, and otherwise varied, attested the boundless fertility of the feminine mind, when let loose in a given direction."

pie in the sky. An empty wish or promise. The expression may have originated with a song written by IWW (International Workers of the World) organizer Joe Hill, whose real name was Joseph Hilstrom, in the years before World War I. Called "The Preacher and the Slave" four of its lines went:

> "You will eat, by and by,
> In that glorious land above the sky
> (way up high!);

> Work and pray, live on hay,
> You'll get pie in the sky when you die" (That's a lie!)

Piedmont rice. An old story holds that Thomas Jefferson stole seeds of Piedmont rice while traveling in the Piedmont region of Italy and smuggled them home in his pockets, despite the fact that Italy wanted to continue its monopoly on this type of rice and had made the crime of stealing the seeds punishable by death. Jefferson's introduction of the rice was important because Piedmont rice can be grown without irrigation.

Pimm's. The gin-based British drink was named for London bartender James Pimm after he invented it in 1840. There are now several variations on the original, which is called Pimm's No. 1. All are often mixed with ginger ale or lemonade and served with ice.

pineapple. The Spanish conquistadores named this fruit *piña* because of its pine-cone shape and the English translated *pina* to *pineapple,* which they also called the cones of the pine tree.

pizza. One of America's favorite foods, pizza is also one of its most recent treats, the word pizza not recorded in the U.S. until 1935. Pizza's ultimate origins are unknown. One theory holds it comes from Italian *pizza* (or *pitta*) for the same, with the Italian word deriving from an unknown Greek word. Another theory has pizza coming from Italian *pizzicare,* "to pinch or pluck," in reference to the making of a pizza pie. The term *pizzeria* was first recorded in 1943, while *pizza parlor* appeared in print about five years later. In some regions, including New York, *slice* is the word to use when ordering a piece of pizza. Other places use *piece* exclusively. A *Neopolitan* pizza is the classic thin-sliced pizza, while a *Sicilian* pizza is a square, thick pie. In England a pizza parlor is called a *pizza bar.*

plum. The Old English *plume,* derived from the Greek *proumnon* for the fruit, gives us the English word *plum.* Burbank plums are probably the most famous in America, and take their name from the noted plant breeder Luther Burbank, who developed some 60 varieties of plums besides the Burbank. The Damson plum, another favorite, is named for the place where it originated; according to tradition, Alexander the Great first brought it to Greece from Damascus, Syria; the Romans called it the plum of Damascus, *prunum damas cenum,* which became *damascene plum* and finally *damson plum* in English. The renowned Greengage plum, which is actually yellow with a tinge of green, was brought from Italy to France in about 1500, where it was named the *Reine-Claude* after Claudia, *la bonne reine,* queen to Francis I.

About 1725, Sir William Gage, an amateur English botanist, imported a number of plum trees from a monastery in France, all of which were labeled except the Reine-Claude. A gardener named the unknown variety after his employer, and the Reine-Claude has been the greengage in England and America ever since. *See* POLITICAL PLUM.

plum pudding dog. This was once a common name for the Dalmatian, or spotted coach dog, breed. The Dalmatian pointer was called the plum pudding dog because of its mottled appearance, its spots being like the plums or raisins in a pudding; the term was first recorded in 1897.

political plum. When a delighted Matthew S. Quay was elected U.S. senator from Pennsylvania in 1887, he assured his supporters that he would "shake the plum tree" for them. From this promise came our expression *a political plum,* an excellent or desirable thing, a fine job. The Little Jack Horner who pulled out a plum from the pie may have contributed to the term's popularity.

pomato. *Pomato* was first used by Luther Burbank in 1905 for the fruit of a hybrid potato, but his creation didn't catch on, and *pomato* later became the name of the potato-tomato plant, with the potatoes growing underground on the roots of the plant and the tomatoes growing above the ground on the plant branches or vines. The chief draw-back for this novelty is that pota-toes can transfer several diseases to tomatoes and viceversa, which is the reason potato fields on farms are generally widely separated from tomato fields. One of the earliest experiments with tomatoes, in 1910, produced a tomato-eggplant chi-mera having characteristics of each parent on the same branch. Many such experiments have been made. At North Carolina State University, for example, tomatoes were grafted on tobacco plant roots. The result was a tomato with a high nicotine content.

pomegranate; garnet; grenade. Commonly called "Chinese apples" in America, *pomegranates,* "the fruit of the ancients," take their name from the Latin for "many-seeded apple." The thick-skinned red fruit, about the size of an orange, is divided into numerous cells inside, each containing many seeds encased in a crimson, juicy pulp. When the fruit is eaten raw, it is broken open and the red flesh is sucked out. Today in the Orient when a newly married couple reaches their new home, pomegranates are broken at the doorway, their crimson-coated seeds signifying both the loss of vir-ginity and an omen that many off-spring will come of the marriage. A number of other words derive from the pomegranate with its red skin and seeds. Our *grenade,* a weapon first used in the late 16th century,

comes from the French *grenade,* a shortening of French *pomegrenade,* for pomegranate. It was originally filled with grains or "seeds" of pow-der and thus facetiously named after the many-seeded fruit. Today the word is used in *hand grenade,* which isn't filled with grains of powder anymore, but can create a scene of carnage as bloody as any shattered pomegranate where it explodes. The military *grenadier,* originally for a soldier who threw grenades, evolved in much the same way from the French shortening, as did the term *grenadine* for the drink made from the fruit. But the garnet stone, its color similar to the flesh of the fruit, was given its name by the Romans, the Latin *granatum* (from *Punic granatum* or Punic apple: the pomegranate) becoming *grenat* in Old French and shifting by metathesis to *garnet* in English over the years.

popcorn. Certainly known to the Aztecs, popcorn was so named by American settlers on the frontier in the early 19th century. It is a vari-ety of small-eared corn (*Zea mays everta*), the kernels of which pop open when subjected to dry heat and has also been called "parching corn," "popped corn," "pot corn," "cup corn," "dry corn," and "buck-shot" over the years. The great quan-tities of it sold in movie theaters prompted some early movie house corporations to grow thousands of acres of popcorn.

popsicle. The popsicle might still be an "Epsicle" if Frank W. Epperson (1894–1983) hadn't gone broke in 1929 and sold his patent for his "handled, frozen confection or ice lollipop" to a small company, which changed its name from *Epsicle* to *Popsicle*. Epperson had dubbed his successful product the Epsicle some 19 years after he accidentally invented it one cold San Francisco night in 1905, when as an 11-year-old he left a glass of lemonade on his porch and "awoke the next morning to find the drink frozen solid around a spoon that was in it."

port wine. This sweet red dessert wine is named port, the word first recorded in 1591, because it was first shipped to England from the town of Oporto in northern Portugal. Its types include vintage port, tawny port, ruby port, and white port (made from white grapes).

porterhouse steak. Martin Morrison's Porterhouse in New York City introduced the porterhouse steak in about 1814, according to the *Dictionary of Americanisms*. The tender steak taken from the loin next to the sirloin is an even more succulent cut than its neighbor, but has a lot of waste. In England, there is generally no distinction between it and sirloin. A porterhouse was a tavern serving the dark brown beer or ale called porter, once favored by porters and other laborers.

potato. The white potato is one of the most important vegetables in the world, yet it bears the wrong name. *Potato* derives from the Haitian word *batata,* for "sweet potato," which the Spanish found in the West Indies in 1526 and introduced to Europe. *Batata* was corrupted to *patata* in Spanish, and this altered to *potato* when first used in England. But then the Spaniards discovered the Peruvian white potato, an unrelated plant, and mistook it for just another variety of the West Indian plant. Ignoring the native name for the white potato, *papas,* they gave it the same name as the earlier tuber, and so it too became known as the *potato* in England. The only distinction between the two unrelated vegetables was that one came to be called the *sweet potato* and the other the *Virginia* or *white potato.* The white potato is called "apple of the earth," *pomme de terre* in French, and "earth-apple," *Erdapfel* in German. It acquired the name *Irish potato* when it was first brought to this country in 1719 by a group of Irish Presbyterians and planted in Londonderry, New Hampshire. The colloquial American name *spud* for it derives from the spade-like tool used in digging potatoes. The humorous *Murphy* derives from the wide consumption of potatoes in Ireland—where there are of course many Murphys—at a time when other European countries rarely used the tuber for anything but fodder.

potato chip. George Crum, a Saratoga, New York cook of partial American Indian descent, is said to have invented potato chips in 1853 when a patron in the restaurant where he worked complained that the potatoes he had been served were too thick and undercooked. Crum sliced some potatoes paper thin, soaked them in ice-water and fried them in a kettle of boiling oil. According to the old story, the customer raved about them, they became a specialty of the restaurant and were soon dubbed potato chips.

power lunch. A lunch attended by at least two powerful people, often movers and shakers of society, people who can get things done. The power lunch is said to have been born in the Grill Room of the Four Seasons restaurant in New York City, or at least to have been so named there. The Four Seasons, designed by Philip Johnson, opened in 1959 and is considered an "interior landmark" of New York City.

prairie oysters; mountain oysters. tn a country where the prudish have called the bull "a cow's father," "a cow creature," "a male cow," "a Jonathan," and "a gentleman cow," it is no wonder that there are so many euphemisms for bulls' testicles. In French and Spanish restaurants bulls' balls are sometimes called just that on the menus, but in America, when they are offered, they're invariably labeled either "prairie oysters," "mountain oysters," "Rocky Mountain oysters," or "Spanish kidneys." Believed to be an elevating aphrodisiac dish despite their low origins, bulls' balls are probably no more than a psychological aphrodisiac. But French neurologist Charles Brown-Dequard, who founded the much disputed "science" of organotherapy in 1889, thought differently. He claimed that both he and his patients had greatly enhanced their sexual prowess by eating bulls' testicles. The 70-year-old scientist went so far as to transplant bulls' testicles under the abdominal walls of patients, but it has since been established that testicles cannot store sex hormones such as testosterone and that when transplanted they wither and die.

pretzel. There is no proof that pretzels are twisted to represent "the folded arms of praying children," as is often claimed, and they certainly don't take their name from the Latin *pretiola*, "little reward," because they were given by monks to religiously faithful children. Why they are twisted no one really knows, and the word *pretzel*, first recorded here in 1824, in a reference to pretzels eaten by the Dutch, derives from the German word for "branch," in reference to the branches of a tree that the "arms" of the pretzels resemble.

pumpkin. This member of the squash family originated in the Americas, where pumpkins were so ubiquitous among the Pilgrims that

some wit wrote the following: "We have pumpkins at morning and pumpkins at noon, / If it were not for pumpkins we would soon be undoon." The pumpkin didn't get its name because it looks "pumped up" into a balloon shape. *Pumpkin* probably comes from the Greek *pepon,* a kind of melon, literally, "a fruit cooked by the sun." *Pepon* became the Middle French *ponon,* which became the English *pompion,* to which the diminutive suffix-kin was finally added. It is just another example of the many English words formed from mispronunciations of foreign words. Seneca is said to have written a satire on the deification of the Roman emperor Claudius Caesar, which he called *Apocolocyntosis,* coined from the Greek word for pumpkin and meaning "pumpkinification" *Pumpkinification,* suggesting a swollen head the size of a pumpkin and "pumped up," has meant pompous behavior or absurd glorification since at least the mid-19th century, when a British writer called attention to Seneca's satire.

punch. Legend has it that our beverage *punch* derives from the Hindi *panch,* "five," because it originally had five ingredients: arrack, tea, lemon, sugar, and water. More likely the word comes from the *puncheon,* or large cask, from which grog was served to sailors in the East India trade. In any event, the Indian beverage was a great favorite with sailors and was brought back to England in the late 1600s.

quiche. A quiche is a pielike dish made of custard flavored with cheese, onion, bacon, or other ingredients that are baked in an unsweetened pastry shell. The word came into French from the German *Kuche*, "little cake," and seems to have been first recorded in English late in the 19th century.

quicker than you can cook asparagus. Some old-timers still call asparagus *grass*, from the homely expression *sparrow-grass* commonly used as a name for the vegetable over the last three centuries. Asparagus is a Latin word formed from the Greek for sprout or shoot. The Romans cultivated it as early as 200 B.C., growing some stalks at Ravenna that weighed a full three pounds and gathering stems in the Getulia plains of Africa that were actually 12 feet tall. The most flavorful "grass," however, is thin and tender and should be cooked in as little water and as rapidly as possible. Even the Romans knew this, and their Emperor Augustus originated the old saying, *quicker than you can cook asparagus*, for anything he wanted done within a few moments. Asparagus has been regarded as a phallic symbol since earliest times, but this certainly isn't why perennial patches of it are called *beds*, which is just a common garden term. There is an interesting true story about blanched white asparagus, however. Reported a *New York Times* correspondent at a recent Bonn dinner party: "A certain guest complimented the elegant German hostess and said, 'This white asparagus is as beautiful as an undressed woman,' thereby probably becoming the first asparagus eater to have noted a resemblance between asparagus and the attributes of the *female* sex."

quey calves are dear veal. A quey is a female calf, that is, a valuable calf that will one day give milk. To kill such a calf for veal would be foolish, which gives us this old saying similar to *killing the goose that lays the golden egg.*

R

rabage. This unfortunate vegetable is quite real but won't be found in any gardening books or seed catalogs. The rabage (*Raphanobrassica*) is a cross between a radish and a cabbage developed by a Soviet geneticist named Alexi Karpenchinko in 1924. What was expected was a plump head of cabbage on an edible round root of radish. Sadly, what developed was a head of scraggly radish leaves and the thin, useless roots of a cabbage. *See* RADISH.

radish. The easy-to-grow radish (*Raphanus sativus*) takes its scientific name from its Greek name, *raphanes*, "easily reared." Radish itself comes from the Latin *radix*, "root." The Greeks so valued the radish that they made small replicas of radishes in gold, while creating images of their other vegetables in lead or silver. The French call the radish by the poetic name

roses d'hiver, "roses of winter." *See* RABAGE.

rasher of bacon. The *rasher* in this British term, sometimes heard in America, means a slice and probably didn't get its name because it is cooked *rashly* or "quickly." *Rasher* here is more likely a corruption of *rasure,* "a thin slice or shaving."

raspberry. Known to the Romans as the "Red Berry of Mount Ida" (hence the name of the British species *Rubus idaeus*) for Mount Ida in Greece, the raspberry takes its name from the English *rasp*, "to scrape roughly," in reference to the thorned canes bearing the berries. Raspberries have not been cultivated for nearly as long as fruits like apples, peaches, and pears. Called a brambleberry or hindberry and considered a nuisance in England, it was not until about 1830 that the delicate, delicious fruit began to be developed in America. The *Fanny Heath* variety is a tribute to a determined pioneer woman who immigrated to North Dakota in 1881. This young bride had been told that she could never grow anything on the barren alkaline soil surrounding her house, but 40 years later her homestead was an Eden of flowers, fruits, and vegetables. After her death in 1931, the black raspberry she developed was named in her honor. A red raspberry variety honoring a famous person is the *Lloyd George*, named after British prime minister David Lloyd George (1863–1945), who led Britain to victory in World War I and dominated British politics in the first quarter of the 20th century. *Raspberry* meaning a BRONX CHEER, a rude vibrating of the lower lip, derives from British rhyming slang *raspberry tart*, which means "fart" and is at least a century old.

redeye dish gravy. Made from the frying-pan juice of country ham, thickened with flour and frequently containing a little coffee for color and flavor; also called redeye gravy.

Restaurant Into Which You Would Not Take a Dog. This is the name of a Shanghai restaurant, in a country far removed from hype, where eating establishments often vie with one another in coining self-deprecating names for themselves. Other examples include The Second-Class Establishment of Mr. Hsiang and Enter Here If Your Must.

Reuben. No one is sure who invented this grilled sandwich of corned beef, Swiss cheese, sauerkraut, and Russian dressing on rye bread. The best guess is that it was first concocted at Reuben's Delicatessen in Manhattan during the early 1900s.

Revenge is a dish that tastes best when it is cold. An old Italian proverb that is a favorite of the Godfather, Don Corleone, in Mario Puzo's novel *The Godfather* (1969). A pithier variation is *Revenge is a dish best served cold.*

rhubarb. Speculation has been rife for years about how the slang term *rhubarb*, "a heated argument," arose from the name of a popular vegetable. Since the word is often associated with baseball, many writers say it has its origins there. But probably the best explanation, advanced about 25 years ago by a veteran actor familiar with theatrical traditions, is that actors simulating angry talk in crowd scenes for "the noise without" gathered backstage and "intoned the sonorous word 'rhubarb.'" The actor-etymologist Alexander McQueen advised that the word produces such an effect "only if two or three work at it," and claimed that this theatrical tradition went back to Shakespearean times, but the slang *rhubarb* for an argument arose only in the late 19th century. It therefore came to mean a "rumpus" or a "row" at about the time baseball was fast becoming America's national pastime. It is easy to see how the stage term could have been applied to an argument on the diamond, especially a mass argument that involved both teams, though there is no solid proof of this. *Rhubarb* itself has an interesting derivation, taking its name from the Latin *rha barbarum*. The Romans called it this because the plant was native to the river Rha (the Volga), a foreign, "barbarian" territory—the plant's name, thus meaning "from the barbarian (foreign) Rha." The first rhubarb planted in America was sent to the great naturalist John Bartram from Siberia in 1770. Americans long called the fruit pieplant because it made such delicious pies, especially when combined with strawberries.

road pizza. Roadkill is common but road pizza is one on me. According to journalist Marion McKeone, writing in William Safire's *On Language* column (July 30, 2006), a New York cop shouted it when a pedestrian tried to cross the street against the light: "Whassamatterwichya? Ya wanna be road pizza, ya (expletive) moron?"

rocky road. The variety of ice cream, consisting of chunks of chocolate ice cream, marshmallows, and almonds, was originally the name of a candy bar in the Great Depression years. Both the candy and the ice cream that took its name were meant to symbolize the rocky road people had before them in hard times, making the hard times easier by joking about them.

romaine lettuce. The French believed that this tall, upright lettuce with ribbed leaves was first cultivated by the Romans and named it *latique* (lettuce) *romaine*, soon shortening this to "romaine" alone. But the lettuce is also called Cos, after the Greek island where some botanists say the variety was first grown centuries ago.

rubber chicken. An unappetizing dish invariably on the menu at dinners, banquets, and other large gatherings in the U.S. The British equivalent is *function fish*.

rutabaga; Swedish turnip. Commonly called the Swedish turnip, the rutabaga derives its name from the Swedish dialect *rotabagge*, for the plant; this relatively new vegetable, first recorded in 1620, is extensively grown in Sweden. It is also called Swede.

Sacher torte. History's most famous chocolate cake is named for 19th-century Austrian confectioner Edward Sacher. Sacher, whose cigar-smoking mother served her son's creation to Prince Metternich, actually won a lawsuit from a rival confectioner over who could legally call the cake his own. The cake is made of chocolate torte batter, apricot jam, and chocolate frosting.

saffron. Saffron costs about $400 a pound, making it one of the world's most expensive spices. This is primarily because it takes 4,000 blossoms of the autumn crocus (*Crocus sativus*), or 225,000 of its handpicked stigmas, to make one ounce of saffron. But luckily a little goes a long way, for the spice has been coveted by gourmets and lovers since the Arabs introduced it to Spain in the eighth century A.D. Even before then saffron was used by the Phoenicians to flavor the moon-shaped love cakes dedicated to Astoreth, their goddess of fertility. Today the spice is often called "vegetable gold." The old expression *he hath slept in a bed of saffron* refers to the supposed exhilarating effects of saffron, meaning "he has a very light heart." As an old poem puts it:

> With genial joy to warm his soul,
> Helen mixed saffron in the bowl.

St. Patrick's cabbage. Though native to Spain, Saint Patrick's cabbage (*Saxifrage umbrosa*) is found in the mountains of west Ireland as well, for which reason it is named for St. Patrick, archbishop of Armagh, the apostle of Ireland. This ornamental with crimson-spotted petals is also known as London Pride. St. Patrick is said to be responsible for the shamrock being the Irish national emblem. When captured by a pagan ruler while preaching in the country he plucked a shamrock and explained that its three leaves were distinct and separate on the plant, "just as the Trinity is the union of three distinct persons in One Deity."

salad days. Cleopatra, kidded by Charmian about her old love for Julius Caesar, joked that those were her *salad days* salad days when she was "green in judgement, cold in blood." In other words she loved Caesar unskillfully and without much passion compared to the way she loved Mark Antony. Thus our expression for naive and inexperienced youth comes to us from Shakespeare's *Antony and Cleopatra.* The real Cleopatra was actually a flaming youth, a trained and artful lover before her adolescence, and the *salad days* that Shakespeare has her admit to were distant memories long before she married her brother at 17.

Salisbury   steak;   hamburger. *Hamburger* literally signifies an inhabitant of Hamburg, the great German seaport, the *Hamburg steak* originating there, but *Salisbury steak,* a hamburger without a bun, derives from the name of a 19th-century English physician, Dr. James H. Salisbury. Salisbury steak, as every Army veteran knows, is really something more, or less, than a hamburger. The "steak" part makes it

look good on menus, but today it is usually either a well-done hamburger, or a combination of ground beef, eggs, milk and bread crumbs cooked in patties and drowned in a gooey gravy.

Salisbury steak started out as well-done hamburger alone. In 1888 Dr. Salisbury advised his patients to eat well-cooked ground beef three times a day, with hot water before and after each feast. This diet, the health faddist claimed over the laughter of his colleagues, would either cure or relieve pulmonary tuberculosis, hardening of the arteries, gout, colitis, asthma, bronchitis, rheumatism, and pernicious anemia.

During World War I and again in World War II, efforts were made to drive German loan words like *hamburger* out of the language, a *hamburger steak* becoming a *Salisbury steak* and a *hamburger* a *liberty sandwich*. These efforts by superpatriots didn't succeed. One suspects that *Salisbury steak* only survived

because it made an excellent euphemism for hamburger. Certainly no one eats ground beef and hot water for health reasons anymore.

salmagundi. The origin of the word is really unknown. A *salmagundi,* "any mixture or miscellany," began as a mishmash of minced veal, chicken, or turkey, anchovies or pickled herring, and onions served with lemon juice and oil. One theory has it that the word comes from *salame condite,* Italian for "pickled meat"; another that it derives from the name of a lady-in-waiting to Marie de' Medici, wife of France's Henri IV. Marie is supposed to have invented the eclectic dish, or made it de rigueur at least, and named it after Madame or Ma de moi selle Salmagundi, her lady-in-waiting. Later the word was used by Washington Irving for a series of 20 periodical pamphlets that he and two other writers published (1807–08). *Salmagundi; or the Whim-Whams and Opinions of Launcelot Langstaff , Esq. and others,* consisted of satirical essays and poems on New York society and politics, generally satirizing "mobocratic" and "Logocratic" Jeffersonian democracy.

salmon. The often pink-fleshed fish (from the Latin *salmon*) gives its name to the color salmon, but the salmon's flesh doesn't have to be pink—in fact, it is frequently white. Nevertheless, many Americans believe that salmon should be pink to be good. Over half a century ago the legendary advertising genius Elmer Wheeler (he coined the slogan "Don't sell the steak—sell the sizzle") was hired by a West Coast salmon cannery to get people to eat the white variety and learn that it is just as tasty. Wheeler had new labels pasted on every can of the company's huge stock, each of them bearing the slogan: this salmon guaranteed not to turn pink in the can.

Salmonella. Salmon have no connection with *Salmonella* or *salmonellosis.* The latter is a form of food poisoning that can result in death and is caused by bacteria of the *Salmonella* genus, comprising some 1,500 species. The *Salmonella* genus was first identified by 19th-century American pathologist and veterinarian Daniel Elmer Salmon, who died in 1914. There are often outbreaks of salmonellosis, which is usually caused by infected and insufficiently cooked beef, pork, poultry, and eggs, as well as food, drink, or equipment contaminated by the excreta of infected animals. Nearly all animals are hospitable to the rodshaped bacteria causing the acute gastroenteritis in humans, and food poisoning caused by them are almost as common as those caused by staphylococci. Incidentally, there is a "salmon disease" dogs and other animals get from eating salmon infested with cysts of flukes, but it has nothing to do with salmonellosis.

salt. In ancient times salt was highly valued, so much so that spilling salt became an unlucky omen among the Romans. Roman soldiers were in fact paid in salt, (*sal*) at one time, the origin of our word *salary*. Through the centuries a number of expressions reflected the importance of the precious seasoning and preservative. "Not worth his salt" referred to the salary the Romans paid their soldiers; "to eat a man's salt" meant to partake of his hospitality; and "to sit above the salt" was to sit in a place of distinction, above the saler, or saltcellar, at a medieval table. "The salt of the earth" is an even older saying, dating back to biblical times. In Matt. 5:13 the meek, the poor in spirit, the merciful, those persecuted for the sake of righteousness, the peacemakers, the pure of heart are told by Jesus that "Ye are the salt of the earth . . . Ye are the light of the world." The words are still a supreme compliment given to those we most admire as human beings.

salt a mine. To secretly stock a gold, silver, or diamond mine with ore or precious stones to make it appear valuable. The expression is said to derive from the practice of dishonest miners scattering a handful of salt, which is the color of gold dust, through mines they wished to sell to unwary investors.

salt horse. Beef or pork pickled in brine was often called *salt horse* on the New England coast and elsewhere. An old rhyme went:

"Old horse! old horse! what
 brought you here?"
"From Sacarap to Portland Pier
I've carted stone for many a year;
Till, killed by blows and sore
 abuse,
They salted me down for sailor's
 use.
The sailors they do me despise,
They turn me over and damn my
 eyes;
Cut off my meat and scrape my
 bones
And heave the rest to Davy Jones."

The "Sacarap" in the verse was a part of Westbrook, Maine, near Portland Pier, but the term *salt horse* is probably English in origin.

saltwater taffy. The traditional story here has a storm and flood striking near the Atlantic City boardwalk, ruining the sweet chewy taffy the owner had left overnight in his candy stand. Not to be bested, the candyman sold his wares as saltwater taffy, which it remains today, a little sea water used in its preparation. All we really know is that the first printed mention of saltwater taffy is 1910.

saltimbocca. This Italian veal and ham dish looks so delicious that some poetic gastronome several centuries ago named it *saltimbocca:* "leaps into the mouth."

sandwich. At 5 a.m. on August 6, 1762, John Montagu, fourth earl of Sandwich, looked up from the gaming table and decided that he was hungry. The earl, an inveterate gambler in the midst of one of his famous round-the-clock sessions, didn't dare leave his cards for a meal and ordered his man to bring him some cold, thick-sliced roast beef between two pieces of toasted bread. Thus the first sandwich was born. The Romans had a similar repast called *offula* before this, and it is said that the refreshment was first invented when in about 100 B.C. Hillel ate bitter herb and unleavened bread as part of the Jewish Passover meal, symbolizing man's triumph over life's ills. But the modern sandwich, our convenient quick lunch or snack and an important source of nourishment in this frenetic age, definitely evolves from those mighty gambling sessions, some lasting 48 hours and more, in which the dissolute earl passionately participated. Gambling was one of John Montagu's lesser vices, but the earl has as many words honoring him as any politician, another example being the beautiful Sandwich Islands (Hawaii) that Captain James Cook named after him because the earl headed the British admiralty during the American Revolution and outfitted the great explorer's ship.

sandwich generation. A term coined about 2001 meaning the generation that is presently sandwiched between the responsibilities of raising their children and caring for their elderly parents.

Sanka. Sanka, a brand of decaffeinated coffee, is a trademark, and must be capitalized. The name of the product, first marketed in 1903, was coined from the French *san*(s) *ca*(ffeine), "without caffeine."

sashimi. Another Japanese word that has recently come intact into the English vocabulary. *Sashimi* means thinly sliced raw fish, which is eaten that way, often with sauces and seasonings.

sausage. *Sausage* comes ultimately from the Latin word *salus,* meaning salted or preserved. This meat treat was invented centuries ago by the Chinese, but the planetary record for the biggest sausage ever made was long held by bakers in Scunthorpe, England. Some years ago they reportedly made the Great Scunthorpe Sausage from this recipe: "Take up 738 pounds of ground pork and work in cereal to extend the mixture to 896 pounds. Take salt, pepper and sage and season to taste. Blend into mixture and force into 3,124 feet of sausage casing (pig intestines). Will serve 6,248." However, today *The Guinness Book of World Records* (1998) gives the title to a Canadian butcher shop that in 1995 made a "continuous sausage" 28.77 *miles* long.

scallion. Crusaders returning from the Holy Land probably introduced the word *scallion* to Europe. These small onions were raised in the Palestinian seaport of Ascalon, now just ancient ruins, and had been named *Ascalonia caepa,* "Ascalonion onion," by the Romans. This was shortened to *scalonia* in the common speech of the Romans and passed into English as *scalyon,* which finally became *scallion. See also* ONION.

scone; high tea. News about the proper pronunciation of scone. R. W. Apple Jr. reports in the *New York Times* (June 11, 2003) that the name of the delicious treat "rhymes with 'prawn,' not with 'bone.'" Mr. Apple also points out that "contrary to widespread American belief, afternoon tea . . . is not 'high tea.' High tea is a heartier, working-class meal usually served about 6 P.M."

sell like hot cakes. Hot cakes cooked in bear grease or pork lard were popular from earliest times in America. First made of cornmeal, the griddle cakes or pancakes were of course best when served piping hot and were often sold at church benefits, fairs, and other functions. So popular were they that by the beginning of the 19th century *to sell like hot cakes* was a familiar expression for anything that sold very quickly, effortlessly, and in quantity.

sesame seeds. *Sesamum indicum* is said to be the oldest herbaceous plant cultivated for its seeds. *Benne,* as these sesame seeds are called in Africa and the South, or *sim sim,* another African name for them, were brought to America on the first

slave ships. They have been used for everything from ink to cattle feed to flour to oil, and are a popular ingredient in cookies, crackers, and candies. *Sesamum* is the Greek version of the Arabic word for sesame.

shaddock. The ancestor of the grapefruit, the shaddock, or pomelo, reached Europe in about the middle of the 12th century from the Malay archipelago. It was called the Adam's apple at first and didn't receive its common name until a Captain Shaddock, a 17th-century English voyager, brought its seed from the East Indies to Barbados, where it was grown extensively. The grapefruit (*Citrus paradisi*) is neither a mutation of the thicker-skinned shaddock (*C. grandis*) nor a cross between the shaddock and sweet orange. It was developed in the West Indies and was given its name because it often grows in clusters like grapes. To further complicate matters, the shaddock is sometimes called the forbidden fruit and the grapefruit is called the pomelo in different parts of the world. The pink grapefruit was developed in Florida, as was the seedless variety.

shadow potatoes. An interesting name Fanny Farmer's *Boston Cookbook* (1909) gives for very thin potato chips.

sherry. Via an indirect route, *sherry* is still another word that derives from Caesar's name. Sherry is made in

Jerez de la Frontera, Spain, for which it was named, and *Jerez* in turn, commemorates Julius Caesar, having originally been called Xeres, this an adaptation of the Latin *urbs Caesaris,* "the town of Caesar." Sixteenth-century Spaniards pronounced Jerez something like *sherris,* which the English adopted and changed to *sherry* because they believed *sherris* was a plural form. Shakespeare wrote "a good sherris-sack hath a twofold operation in it" in *Henry IV, Part II,* but today the false singular is always used. It is said that when Sir Francis Drake burned the port of Cádiz in 1587, he seized 2,500 butts of sherry from nearby Jerez. Drake called the wine *sack,* according to the old folk story, but the dockers unloading the barrels noted the letters XERES (for Jerez) on them and became the first to use the word *zherry,* or *sherry.*

shrimp. Short people are *not* called shrimps because they resemble the shellfish in size. As with sharks, it is the other way around. The common little Europe an species *Crago vulgaris* was named *shrimp* from the Middle English word *shrimpe,* which meant a puny person.

silver spoon. The earliest spoons were made of wood, the word *spoon,* in fact, deriving from the Anglo-Saxon *spon,* "a chip of wood." Until the 19th century most people used pewter spoons, but traditionally, especially among the wealthy, godparents have given the gift of a silver

spoon to their godchildren at christening ceremonies. The custom is centuries old throughout Europe and inspired the saying "born with a silver spoon in one's mouth," *i.e.,* born to hereditary wealth that doesn't have to be earned. This expression is not of American origin as the *O.E.D.* implies; the great dictionary only traces the phrase back to 1800 here, but it is much older, for Cervantes used it in *Don Quixote* (1605–1615): "Every man was not born with a silver spoon in his mouth." The duke of Bedford gave a nice twist to the phrase in the title of his biography, *A Silver-Plated Spoon.* The *silver shoon* in Walter de la Mare's poem "Silver" are "silver shoes," *shoon* being an old plural of *shoe:*

> Slowly, silently, now the moon
> Walks the night in her silver shoon.

sirloin. Sirloin, strictly speaking, is meat from the steer's hip, but today it is sold without the prized filet and often goes by the name of shell hip or rump steak. The widely accepted Sir Loin story about its origins shows how highly esteemed in the past was this aristocrat of steaks. The tale is told about numerous British monarchs, including the lusty Henry VIII, James I (on whom Jonathan Swift bestowed credit), and lastly, Charles II, who ruled England from 1660 to 1685. In each case the king in question was supposed to have been so pleased with the succulent slice of pink meat served him that he unsheathed his sword, laid it on the brown-crusted sirloin and knighted it, solemnly declaring, "Hereafter thou shalt be dubbed 'Sir Loin.'" The only bothersome fact is that *sirloin* really derives from an Old English word *surloin* (from *sur,* "above" or "over"), which simply meant the cut above the loin and came to be misspelled *sirloin* in about 1600. This, however, did not prevent writers like Scott from using terms like *the knightly sirloin* and the *noble baron of beef.* The last, practically unheard of today, was a double sirloin, a huge joint weighing up to 100 pounds and comprising both sides of the back. *See also* PORTER HOUSE.

slice. Often used by Americans instead of a piece of pizza when ordering pizza in a pizzeria or pizza parlor: "Gimme a slice anna small coke." When a whole pizza pie is ordered it's "Gimme a pie." This word is first recorded in the United States in the early 1930s, when slices weren't widely sold as they are today and pies prevailed, these usually eaten at a table in an Italian restaurant. It should be noted that while thinner pieslice-shaped Neopolitan pizza can be asked for by ordering a slice, a square cut of thick Sicilian pizza shouldn't be: "Gimme a piece of Sicilian." Chicago pizza is a deep-dish pizza popular in the Midwest.

a slice off the old ham. Eugene O'Neill's father, James, gave up a promising career as an actor for the financial security of playing the leading role in *The Count of Monte Cristo,* which he played more than 5,000 times. "A chip off the old block, eh?" Eugene said to him soon after he, too, had chosen the theater as a career. "Say, rather, a slice off the old ham," James O'Neill replied.

slick as a peeled onion. An onion peeled of several layers is indeed slick and glistening, which is why this old Americanism is used to describe a slick and slippery person, someone often dishonest.

slime in the ice machine. A recent popular expression or catchphrase in the Houston, Texas, area for anything dirty, icky, gooey, nasty, distasteful. Apparently the expression originated with Houston news broadcaster Marvin Zindler, who uses the words to denounce health violations in local restaurants: "Sliiiiime in the ice machines!" According to the *New York Times* (March 9, 1994), a Texas governor used the same expression publicly when "served a dessert slathered with gooey peach syrup," lending it more prestige.

a small cup of tea. In Kenya this phrase is slang for a bribe or for a "not unreasonable" bribe.

small potatoes. A favorite expression of the character based on big-time crook Meyer Lansky in *The Godfather* (1970), *small potatoes* means "something or someone trivial or insignificant." The term is an Americanism dating back to about 1831, when it was first recorded, and is frequently used in the form *small potatoes and few in a hill*, a favorite Davy Crockett expression. Small potatoes are often called new potatoes and salad potatoes in the U.S. They are usually considered tastier than larger specimens.

smart apple. A wise guy or smart aleck is a *smart apple* today, but when it originated in the early 1920s the term meant an intelligent person. An *apple* had simply been a "guy" before this.

smart cookie. "He's a real smart cookie," a doctor recently told me (2003) of another diagnostician, proving that the expression is still used. The *cookie* in the phrase is American slang for a person and is first recorded in this sense about 1917 in the form of "He's a hardboiled cookie," by hardboiled cookie President Harry S. Truman in his book *Dear Bess*. The expression *smart cookie* in its entirety didn't find its way into print until 1955. *Tough cookie* and *rough cookie* are also heard.

snack. Snacks, so named, probably, because they are quickly "snatched," have meant "mere bites or morsels of food, as contrasted with regular meals" since the 17th century. Wrote the first writer known to use the word: "When once a man has got a snack . . . he too often retains a hankering . . ."

soda pop. At the beginning of the 19th century soda water consisted of nothing but water, a little soda, and sometimes a bit of flavoring. Soon someone thought to force gas into the water and to keep it there under pressure, the soda water sparkling and foaming when the pressure is removed and the gas escapes. The soda was kept under pressure in cylinders that came to be called *soda fountains* and were often quite unsafe, for when dropped the pressure inside them could cause a tremendous explosion, which happened once in a while, according to newspapers of the day. At any rate, the sparkling, popping soda that came out of the fountains probably was responsible for the name *pop*, for "soda," long before soda was bottled. *Soda pop* or *pop*, is not recorded in the language, however, until the early 20th century.

soup and fish. Dating back to 19th-century America, this term for formal white-tie dinner clothes probably derives from the obsolete American term *soup and fish*, for a lavish dinner of many courses. *Soup and fish* for an elaborate dinner, in turn, is apparently related to the still common expression *from soup to nuts,* but this last term seems to have been first recorded in the 1920s.

Soup Nazi. A phrase used on the New York–inspired television comedy *Seinfeld* to refer to a real-life soup merchant located in midtown Manhattan. The impatient Soup Nazi is known for supposedly badgering disorganized patrons and for not including the customary piece of bread with an order of soup for customers who take too long to decide what they want. People tolerate his attitude because he reportedly serves outstanding soup.

soup up. To soup up a car is to improve its capacity for speed by enriching its fuel and/or adjusting the engine. This use of the words was first recorded in about 1940. Soup itself is American slang for car or airplane fuel, while to soup up a horse is to inject dope into the animal to make it run faster.

sourdough bread. Now known in commercial forms throughout the United States, sourdough bread, made from sour or fermented dough, was first a mainstay of miners in the early West, who were in fact *sourdoughs* because they carried some of the fermented dough with them from place to place to start new batches of bread.

sour grapes. In Aesop's fable "The Fox and the Grapes," a fox spies luscious-looking grapes hanging from a vine. He leaps a number of times trying to get them, failing by a few inches with each leap, and gives up after rationalizing that they are probably sour and inedible anyway. La Fontaine, another great fabulist, later regarded the fox as admirable, remarking that his words were "better than complaining," but the fox's *sour grapes* have come to mean any belittling, envious remark.

southern fried chicken. Originally chicken fried in bacon grease, southern fried chicken has been popular in the American South since before 1711, when the term *fried chicken* is first recorded there. It became popular throughout the country in the 1930s, when it was first widely sold at roadside restaurants. *See* GOSPEL BIRD.

spaghetti; macaroni. Italian for "little strings, strands, or cords," *spaghetti* was brought to Italy by Marco Polo in the early 14th century and so named at that time, though it is apparently not recorded in English until 1888, the editors of the *O.E.D.* much preferring *macaroni* (first recorded by Ben Jonson in 1599) and not including spaghetti until the first supplement to that masterful work. *Macaroni,* an Italian word of obscure origins, has had its derogatory uses. As early as 1764 *macaroni* meant a fop or a dandy (as in the "Yankee Doodle" lyric), referring o London's Macaroni Club, where the members enjoyed foreign foods like macaroni. Then there is *macaroni boats,* a mostly British term for ocean liners carrying Italian immigrants to America in the early 20th century.

Spam. People all over the world have eaten some 5 billion cans of Spam since the Hormel Foods Corporation began selling it under this name. At first Hormel sold the mixture of pork shoulder, ham, salt, sugar, and sodium nitrate as *special ham.* When other meatpackers began selling the same product, the company in 1936 sponsored a nationwide contest to create a memorable brand name. Actor Kenneth Daigneau, the brother of a Hormel executive, won a mere $100 for *Spam,* which Judith Stone in an exhaustive July 3, 1994, article in the *New York Times Magazine* ("Five Million Cans And Counting") called "arguably the planet's most recognizable portmanteau word" (a combination of the *s* from *shoulder,* the *p* from *pork* and the *am* from *ham*).

However, *chortle* (from *chuckle* and *snort*) may be better known.

spill the beans. A fanciful story, widely printed, holds that members of Greek secret societies voted on the admission of new members by dropping beans into jars or helmets. White beans signified an affirmative vote and black beans a negative ballot. Occasionally, the story says, voters would accidentally knock over the jar or helmet, revealing the secret vote, spilling the beans. However, the phrase is an American one that entered the language only around the beginning of this century. No one knows how it made its entrance, unless it was on the heels of an older expression, as an extension of KNOW BEANS, "to know what is what."

spinach. Popeye did so much for this vegetable with the young set that spinach growers in one Texas town erected a large statue to him. Some authorities claim *spinach* derives from the Latin *hispanicusolus,* "the Spanish herb." The word does come to us from Spain, but probably not directly. Apparently the Persian and Arabian *isfanakh* became the Old Spanish *espinaca,* which eventually changed into the Middle French *espinache,* which resulted in our word *spinach.* At any rate, the Arabs did introduce the vegetable into Spain, and then it spread to the rest of Europe. Dr. Johnson, for one, enjoyed it, according to Boswell. Napoleon did almost as much for spinach's fame as Popeye by decorating the golden epaulettes of his colonels with what looked like gold spinach leaves and were thus referred to as *spinach*— a term that lingers to this day. The phrase *gammon and spinach*, meaning "nonsense," or "humbug," is not as familiar today as it was in Dickens's time, when he wrote in *David Copperfield*, "What a world of gammon and spinnage it is; though, ain't it!" The phrase, most likely an elaboration of the slang word *gammon*, which meant "nonsense" or "ridiculous story," is probably patterned on the older phrase "gammon and patter," the language of London underworld thieves. The nonsense part of it was possibly reinforced by the old nursery rhyme "A Frog He Would A-Wooing Go" (1600), which was heard by millions: "With a rowley powley gammon and spinach / Heigh ho! says Anthony Rowley." E. B. White wrote the caption that became the catchphrase "I say it's spinach, and I say the hell with it" for the Carl Rose cartoon that appeared in the December 8, 1928, issue of *The New Yorker*. It shows a spoiled little girl who rejects her indulgent mother's offer of broccoli with words that have come to mean, "When I'm indulging my prejudices I don't want to be confused with facts." The phrase's abbreviated form, *spinach*, means "baloney," "malarkey," "bull." In 1991 President George Bush joined the ranks of broccoliphobes when he told the press that he hates the stuff. President Clinton has gone on record that he likes it.

steak. *Steak*, an old English word, takes its name from the way such meat was first cooked; on a thin *stake*, from the Old English *staca*, akin to stick. The word is first recorded as *styke* in the early 15th century.

steak tartare. Bloodthirsty about their meals as well as their conquests, the nomadic Tartars liked their meat raw, or almost always so—sometimes they placed a hunk of meat under the saddle and cooked it by friction during hours of riding. At any rate, in medieval times traveling Hamburg merchants learned about a recipe for scraped raw meat seasoned with salt, pepper, and onion juice and named it *tartar steak* or *steak tartare* in their honor. This was the first hamburger, remaining so until some anonymous Hamburger shaped *steak tartare* into patties and cooked them. Tartar sauce, a mayonnaise containing diced pickles, onions, olives, capers, and green herbs, takes its name from tartar steak, which was often seasoned with similar ingredients.

stew. Now the synonym for a brothel or a prostitute, a stew was in medieval times the town bath house. Toward the end of the Middle Ages the town bath house became the gathering place for loose men and women, *stew* taking on its present meaning. Our word *stew* for meat and vegetables slowly boiled together comes from the same source, the verb meaning to bathe in a hot bath or stew.

stove. The first *stoves* were saunas, not kitchen appliances. *Stove* comes to us from the Old English *stofa* "a hot air bath," or sauna, the hot steam baths brought to England from Scandinavia. *Stofa* didn't change in spelling to *stove* until the 15th century and it wasn't until the 16th century that *stove* was used to mean a furnace.

strawberry. Several theories have been proposed about the origin of *strawberry*, but none is convincing. Some say the straw mulch often used in its cultivation inspired the name, others that the dried berries were once strung on straw for decorations, still others that the long runners of the mother plant (strawlike when dry) gave the fruit its name. The word was used as early as A.D. 100 in England and doesn't derive from any other language. It may be that the *straw* in *strawberry* is a corruption of the word *strew*. Certainly the mother plant strews, or scatters, new plants all over a patch when it propagates itself by sending out runners. There's always been an air of mystery surrounding the strawberry. The early Greeks, in fact, had a taboo against eating them, as they did against any red food, and pregnant women in the Middle Ages avoided them because

they believed their children would be born with *strawberry marks* (small, slightly raised birthmarks resembling strawberries) if they did. A *strawberry roan* is a reddish-coated horse flecked with white hair.

strawberry friend. This oldtime rural Americanism describes people who visit from the city when strawberries are in season to get free berries (and other produce) from their rural friends or relatives.

string bean. *String beans* is an Americanism for green beans, first recorded in 1759 and so named for the stringlike fibers along the vegetable sutures. When Burpee & Co. seedsmen developed the Beautiful Burpee, "the stringless string bean," in 1894 the term *string bean* began to take a back seat to *green bean*. It is still heard, however, along with other synonyms like *snap beans* (named for the sound the pods make when broken), *wax beans* (yellow varieties), *kidney beans,* and *haricot*. Napoleon wouldn't eat string beans, afraid that he would choke on the strings.

sugar. The sweetener sugar, made mainly from sugarcane and beet sugar, takes its name from Persian *sukkar* for the same. First recorded as *zuker* in 1299, it has since the 1850s meant "money" and can be a welcome or unwelcome form of address from a man to a woman. *Sugar coat* means "to make something more palatable or acceptable." "Did you know that *sugar* and *sumac* are the only two words in English that begin with *su* and are pronounced *shu?*" historian B. H. Liddell Hart said to George Bernard Shaw. "Sure," replied Shaw.

sushi. Japanese sushi bars have found great popularity in America within the last 30 years, and the word *sushi* has become familiar to many Americans. *Sushi* means "it is sour," referring to the vinegar and other ingredients used in making it. It is often composed of cold rice molded into small pieces and topped with raw seafood (*sashimi*). In sushi bars diners enjoy raw fish like *maguro* (tuna); jellyfish cut into strips like spaghetti; and a kind of shrimp (*ebi*) that is eaten whole still alive and wiggling. Of the *ebi* the Japanese particularly relish a squirming delicacy called *ebi odori*,

which is made by shelling, gutting, and splitting a shrimp down the middle—the creature's nerves are still functioning when it is pressed into a small ball of rice that doesn't stop trembling until it is popped into the mouth.

Swiss chard. Chard is a variety of beet that is cultivated for its leaves and stalks. It apparently takes its name from the French *chardon,* "thistle," a word closely related to the Latin word for thistle. *Swiss chard* is the most famous variety.

Tabasco. The condiment sauce's name, which is a trademark, was apparently first applied to a potent liquor once popular in the American Southwest. The liquor, in turn, took its name from the state of Tabasco in Mexico.

take the cake; cakewalk. Cakes have been awarded as prizes since classical times, so when slaves on southern plantations held dance contests to help a needy neighbor, or just for the fun of it, giving a cake to the winning couple was no innovation. But the cakewalk inspired by these contests was definitely another black contribution to American culture. Dancers tried to outdo each other with fancy steps, struts, and ways of walking while the fiddler played and chanted, "Make your steps, and show your style!" By 1840 *cakewalk* was recorded as the name of these steps, which became the basis of many top dance routines still seen today. Whether the expression *that takes the cake*, "that wins the highest prize," comes from the cakewalk is another matter. Though the phrase is recorded a century earlier elsewhere, it almost certainly originated with the cakewalk in America. Today it has taken on a different meaning and is said of something (or someone) that is so unusual as to be unbelievable. What we know as *cakes*, however, are a comparatively recent innovation. *Fishcakes, pancakes*, and other round comestibles were known long before English cooks began experimenting with the sweet cakes that bear the name today.

take with a grain of salt. Pliny the Elder, who of all ancient historians should most often be taken with a *cellar* of salt, writes that when Pompey seized Mithridates' palace he found the king of Pontus's fabled secret antidote against poisons that had protected him from assassins all his life. It contained 72 ingredients, none of them given by the historian, but the last line of the famous formula supposedly read to "be taken fasting, plus a grain of salt [*addito salis granito*]." The incredulous Pliny isn't known for his subtlety, so it is doubtful that he meant the phrase in any but its literal sense. Nevertheless, the story arose in modern times that Pliny's remark was skeptical and was the origin of the expression *to take with a grain of salt*, "to accept something with reservations, to avoid swallowing it whole." People quoted Pliny's Latin phrase incorrectly and *cum grano salis* was widely accepted as the ancestor of the expression. Actually, the term is little more than three centuries old. Its origin is unknown, and it obviously stems from the idea that salt makes food more palatable and easier to swallow. The Romans knew this, and even sprinkled salt on food they thought might contain poison, but there is no record that they ever used the phrase to indicate skepticism.

talk turkey. According to an old story, back in Colonial days a white hunter unevenly divided the spoils of a day's hunt with his Indian companion. Of the four crows and four wild turkeys they had bagged, the hunter handed a crow to the Indian, took a turkey for himself, then handed a second crow to the Indian and put still another turkey in his own bag.

All the while he kept saying, "You may take this crow and I will take this turkey," or something similar, but the Indian wasn't as gullible as the hunter thought. When he had finished dividing the kill, the Indian protested: "You talk all turkey for you. You never once talk turkey for me! Now I talk turkey to you." He then proceeded to take his fair share. Most scholars agree that from this probably apocryphal tale, first printed in 1830, comes the expression let's talk turkey, "let's get down to real business."

tamale. A dish made of minced, seasoned meat stuffed in cornmeal dough, wrapped in corn husks and steamed; from the Nahuatl *tamalli* for the same.

tangerine. This fruit is called the "kid- glove orange" because its loose skin can be peeled off as easily as soft kid gloves can be peeled off the hands. But it is far better known as the *tangerine* after the seaport Tangier in Morocco, where the small deep-orange fruit was extensively cultivated and first called the "tangerine orange." Tangerines belong to the mandarin group of oranges, which were first cultivated in southeast Asia. Residents of Tangier are called Tangerines. The word *Tangerine* also means a resident of Tangier.

tart. Another example of words that change in meaning. The fruit pie dessert called a tart derives from the Latin *tarta* meaning the same. By at least the 1860s *tart* was being used as a term of endearment for a girl or woman, but after another 20 years, for reasons unknown, it took on its present sense of an immoral woman or prostitute, never to be used endearingly again.

tea. British slang for a cup of tea is "cuppa char." *Char* is a corruption of *cha*, which means tea in England, deriving from the Mandarin *ch'a* for the same. Tea comes to us from the Chinese Amoy dialect *t'e*. The scientific name of the tea plant, *Thea sinensis*, sometimes grown in the United States, is the Latinized version of the Amoy name. Tea bags weren't invented until the turn of the century, when an American tea wholesaler named Sullivan began mailing prospective customers one-cup samples of his tea contained in little silk bags. The idea didn't catch on because the cloth changed the flavor of the tea, but during World War II chemists developed a tasteless paper tea bag that became extremely popular and accounts for most of the tea sold in America today. *See also* ALL THE TEA IN CHINA; TEMPEST IN A TEAPOT.

tearing up the pea patch. Red Barber popularized this southern U.S. expression for "going on a rampage" when he broadcast Brooklyn Dodger baseball games from 1945–55, using it often to describe fights on the field between players. Barber hails from the South, where the expression is an old one, referring to the prized patch of black-eyed peas, which stray animals sometimes ruined.

tempest in a teapot. This saying for "making a big fuss over a trifle," was first *a tempest in a teacup*. It has been traced back only to 1857, but is probably older. Similar early English sayings were "storm in a wash basin" and "a storm in a cream bowl" (1678). For that matter Cicero, as far back as 400 B.C., referred to a contemporary who "stirred up waves in a wine ladle," and he indicated that the expression was ancient *See also* TEA.

tempura. In Japanese cookery tempura is seafood or vegetables dipped in batter and deep-fried. The word, however, is of Portuguese, not Japanese, origin. On Ember Days, which the Portuguese called by the Latin name *Quatuor Tempora*, "the four times of the year," most people in Portugal eschewed meat and ate deep-fried shrimp or other seafood, which came to be called tempura after the holy days. By the early 1540s Portuguese sailors had introduced tempura to Japan.

that and a nickel will buy (or get) you a cup of coffee. Commonly said when information or goods offered by someone is considered of minimal value. Today, we would better say *That and a dollar will buy (or get) you a cup of coffee.*

that's how the cow ate the cabbage. An expression to indicate the speaker is laying it on the line, telling it like it is, getting down to brass tacks—with the connotation of telling someone what he or she needs to know but probably doesn't want to hear. According to Little Rock attorney Alston Jennings, who submitted this southernism to Richard Allen's February 2, 1991, "Our Town" column in the *Arkansas Gazette,* the expression has its roots in a story about an elephant that escaped from the zoo and wandered into a woman's cabbage patch. The woman observed the elephant pulling up her cabbages with its trunk and eating them. She called the police to report that there was a cow in her cabbage patch pulling up cabbages with its tail. When the surprised police officer inquired as to what the cow was doing with the cabbages, the woman replied, "You wouldn't believe me if I told you!"

the tenderloin. In New York City, where the expression originated in the 1870s, the tenderloin was the area from 23rd to 42nd Streets west of Broadway. Gambling and prostitution flourished in this district, giving police officers "luscious opportunities" for graft. In fact, one cop named Williams was so happy to be assigned to the old 29th precinct covering the area

in about 1890 that he said he had always eaten chuck steak but from now on he'd "be eating tenderloin." His remark led to the area being dubbed *the tenderloin,* that name eventually transferred to similar places throughout the country.

three-martini lunch. A business lunch with martinis or other potables that is used as a tax write-off. Who invented the term is unknown, but pundit William Safire, in his *Safire's Political Dictionary* (1978), says South Dakota senator George McGovern popularized the expression when he ran for president in 1972, attacking the three-martini (or "martoonie") lunch as a common example of unnecessary business expense footed by the taxpayer. *See* MARTINI.

a three-minute decision with two minutes for coffee. A decision with little or no importance at all. Heard at a defense secretary Donald Rumsfeld press conference December 16, 2003 Origin uncertain.

thyme. We pronounce the *th* in *thyme* (time) as a *t* because it passed into English from the French with that pronunciation at an early date. Th yme ultimately comes from the Greek *thuo,* "perfume," in reference to the herb's sweet smell.

Toll House cookie. Perhaps America's favorite pastry, or at least cookie, this chocolate chip delicacy was invented in 1930 by pastry chef Ruth Wakefield of the Toll House Inn in Whitman, Massachusetts.

tomato. Those "affected" people who pronounce it "toe-mah-toe" are historically correct. The plant was first called *tomate* in Spain when introduced there from the New World, and even in the early 16th century it was pronounced in three syllables. The o incidentally has no place at all in "tomato," apparently being there because mid-18th-century Englishmen erroneously believed that it should have this common Spanish ending. *Lycopersicon esculentum* has also been called the *wolf apple,* the *wolf peach,* and the *love apple.* The first two designations arose because most Americans thought that tomatoes were poisonous and didn't eat them until about 1830—the tomato *vine* is, in fact, poisonous, the plant a member of the deadly nightshade family. "You say toe-may-toe and I say toe-mah-toe," Cole Porter wrote, and he might have added if he had the space that Americans also pronounce the fruit's name tamater, termater, mater, tomarters, and tomaties, among other variations.

Regional pronunciations of the plural *tomatoes* are even stranger, including tomatoeses, tomatussis, and martisses. *See also* LOVE APPLES.

too many cooks spoil the broth. A proverb from the late 16th century. There are counterparts in many languages, including: *Too many chefs ruin the sauce* (French); *A ship directed by many pi lots soon sinks* (Spanish); and *With too many rowers the ship will crash into a mountain* (Japanese).

Tootsie Roll; Chunky. The still popular Tootsie Roll was invented by American candy maker Leo Hirschfield in 1896. He named the chewy chocolate for his daughter Clara, whose nickname was Tootsie. Another similar named candy is the square hunk of chocolate, cashews, brazil nuts, and raisins called the Chunky. Candy maker Philip Silverstein invented the confection and named it after his daughter, nicknamed Chunky.

top banana. A comic or comedian in American burlesque or vaudeville. The expression derives from an old turn-of-the-century burlesque skit that involved the sharing of bananas.

torpedo juice. Thirsty sailors in World War II sometimes made a potent drink called torpedo juice from alcohol drained from Navy torpedoes. This deadly brew soon lent its name to any raw homemade whiskey with killing power.

tougher than a 30-cent steak. This humorous expression was used in the 1943 movie *Heaven Can Wait* to describe a tough guy. It must date back a century or so, for there were no 30-cent steaks (no matter how tough) available in 1943.

truffle. The "diamonds of gastronomy," as black truffles are called, and the "pearls of the kitchen," white truffles, are the world's most expensive food (save for a few rare spices), selling some years for more than $2,000 a pound. The underground fungi probably take their name from the Osco-Umbrian *tufer*, which is a variation of the Latin *tuber*, "truffle." According to this explanation *tufer* changed to the Vulgar Latin *tufera*, which became by metathesis (the transposing of letters) the Old Provençal *trufa*, which was the basis for the French *truffe* and the English truffle. So far, so good—black truffles, after all, are more plentiful in Italy's Umbria region than anywhere in the world. But why the *l* in truffle? Some authorities believe that it's there because the English *truffle* derives directly from the Swiss *trufla*, not from the French *truffe*. The Swiss word, they claim, comes from the French *truffe*, with the l added from another French word, *trufle*, which means "mockery" or "cheating," alluding to the hard-to-find fungi's habit of hiding

underground. In any event, there was inevitable confusion between the French *truffe* and *trufle*, and it is easy to believe that people accidentally combined the two words, given the truffle's evasive qualities.

It's interesting to note that the eponymous hero of Molière's famous play *Tartuffe* was named for the Italian word for truffles. Tartuffe appears to have been drawn from the character of a bawdy French abbot of the period, and Molière is thought to have used *tartuffe* to symbolize the sensuous satisfaction displayed by certain religious brethren when contemplating truffles. It is said that the name came in a flash to the playwright "on seeing the sudden animation that lighted on the faces of certain monks when they heard that a seller of trufles awaited their orders."

People have always been excited by truffles, so much so that they have gone to the trouble of training many animals with keen senses of smell to sniff them out from under the earth—pigs, dogs, goats, ducks, and even bear cubs among them. No other food has been so eulogized. The "pearl of banquets" has been apostrophized by poets like Pope—"Thy truffles, Périgord!" Porphyrus called truffles "children of the gods"; they were "daughters of the earth conceived by the sun" to Cicero, and "*la pomme féerique*" (the fairylike apple) to George Sand. "Who says 'truffle,'" wrote Brillat-Savarin of the reputed aphrodisiac, "pronounces a grand word charged with toothsome and amorous memories for the skirted sex, and in the bearded sex with memories amorous and toothsome." Perhaps the truffle's aphrodisiac reputation can be explained by the old French proverb, "If a man is rich enough to eat truffles, his loves will be plenty." But aside from this cynical saying, little can be found in any language derogatory of the truffle. About the only such expression is the French slang word *truffle*, which means a "peasant" or "boor," in reference to the peasants of the Périgord and elsewhere who dig for truffles. Truffles are found by gatherers throughout America, though they are inferior varieties and no dogs or pigs are employed to sniff them out. There have been recent successful efforts to farm truffles in Spain.

tuna. An Americanism first recorded in 1884, *tuna* appears to be an anagram of the Spanish *atun*, for the fish, which had been called the tunny (from the Latin *thumis*) in English since at least the 16th century.

tuna fish. There are still thousands of Americanisms that are different from British English expressions, though these have dwindled with the spread of movies, television, and increased foreign travel. A good example of such differences is found in a story about plain old tuna fish. The highest word rate ever paid a screenwriter is the $15,000 producer Darryl F. Zanuck gave American author James Jones for correcting a line of dialogue in the film *The Longest Day*. Jones and his wife, Gloria, were sitting on the beach when they changed the line "I can't eat this bloody old box of tunny fish," to "I can't stand this damned old tuna fish." That works out to three word changes at $5,000 a word.

turkey. The domesticated turkey hardly knows what to eat and has to be attracted to food by colorful marbles placed in its feed; it often catches cold by getting its feet wet and frequently panics and suffocates itself when the flock presses together in fear. For such reasons *turkey* has been slang for any stupid, worthless, useless, unsuitable thing since before 1930. *Turkey* for a poor, third-rate play, movie, or book is said to be an invention of humorist S. J. Perelman, who in the 1920s called himself a "Pennsylvania farmer of prized turkeys, which he displays on Broadway once a year." The word is also used for a socially incompetent, awkward person, a fake drug capsule, easy money (because turkeys are comparatively easy to catch), an easy task (*a turkey shoot*), a valise, a 50-cent piece (from the eagle on the coin), and a hobo's suitcase. *Turkey* comes from *turkey hen*, native to Turkey, which was confused with the American bird.

turnip. *Turnip* comes from the early English *turnepe*, that word blending the noun *turn* (with reference to the vegetable's neatly round shape) and the earlier English word *nepe*, for turnip.

TV dinner. Few people realize that the ubiquitous frozen TV dinner is a trademark name of the C. A. Swanson Company. It was coined in 1953, during the early days of television, when people first began to sit around their TV sets and eat prepared dinners that were easily heated in the oven. It should be added that Gerry Thomas (1922–2005), a Swanson salesman, invented the TV dinner, whose sales now total $30 billion a year.

The first dinner was sold in 1954 and consisted of turkey, peas, sweet potatoes, and cornbread and was served in a compartmentalized tray similar to an army mess kit. *See* TELEVISION.

Twinkie defense. When former San Francisco supervisor Dan White was on trial in 1979 for killing Mayor George Moscone and supervisor Harvey Milk, the defense psychiatrist claimed White's lethal actions were caused by an over-indulgence in junk food such as Twinkies. This came to be called the Twinkie defense. White was paroled after serving five years of his eight-year sentence, but committed suicide 19 months later.

u

ugli fruit. *Ugli* here is simply a spelling variation of *ugly* and is used to describe a large sweet variety of tangelo with rough, wrinkled yellowish skin that originated in Jamaica. A tangelo is a cross between a tangerine and grapefruit. *See* GRAPE.

upper crust. "Kutt the upper crust [of the loaf] for your souerayne [sovereign]," an arbiter of good manners wrote in about 1460. He was referring to the old custom, or proper etiquette, of slicing the choice top crust off a loaf of bread and presenting it to the king or the ranking noble at the table. This practice led to the expression *upper crust,* for "rich or important people," those who ate the upper crust, though this meaning isn't recorded until the mid-19th century.

upset the apple cart. Just as Shakespeare improved the ancient curse *son of a bitch* by making it *son and heir of a mongrel bitch,* some anonymous English wit in the late 18th century transformed an old Roman phrase into *upset the apple cart.* The Roman expression *Perii, plaustrum perculi* ("I am undone, I have upset my cart") meant the same thing, "to ruin carefully laid plans," and might have been changed by some schoolboy who translated the line from Plautus's *Epidicus.* Why the Romans didn't think of using a specific fruit in the expression to make it more graphic is a mystery. They certainly knew all about apples; in fact, the famous French *api* variety of apple (our "Red Lady") is named after the legendary Roman gourmet Apicius, who is said to have produced it by grafting.

vanilla. Vanilla was thought to be wickedly aphrodisiac in Elizabethan England because the pod of the plant resembled the vagina. In fact, the word *vanilla* comes from the Spanish for "little vagina." Queen Elizabeth I used vanilla to flavor her marzipan, making it a favorite flavoring for candy ever since, and Thomas Jefferson was the first to introduce it as a flavoring in America. Today, however, natural vanilla is in short supply and we generally use a synthetic; there isn't enough natural vanilla in the world to flavor the vanilla ice cream made in America alone. Needless to say, natural vanilla is much more flavorsome than the synthetic product. *See* AVOCADO.

vegetable. Vegetables have usually been highly prized, right from the beginning, too, the word *vegetable* itself deriving from the Latin *vegetabilis*, which meant animating or life-giving. The Greeks venerated vegetables, making small gold and silver replicas of the most prized ones. The Roman Fabii, who took their name from the *faba*, or bean; the Piso clan, who derived theirs from the *pisa*, or pea; the *Lentuli*, who named themselves after the *lente*, or lentil; and the great house of Cicero, which took its name from the *cicer*, or chickpea—these are only a few noble Roman families whose patronyms honored widely hailed vegetables.

vegetable lamb. In medieval times the Far Eastern fern *Dicksonia barometz* was thought to be a hybrid animal and vegetable, mainly because of its woolly rootstalk. The down of the plant is used in India to staunch wounds. It is called the *Tartarian* or *Scythian lamb*, as well as the *vegetable lamb*.

venison. *Venison* comes from the Latin *venatio*, "hunting," and was formerly applied to the flesh of any animal killed in the hunt and used as food. The word is first recorded in the early 14th century and gradually came to mean only the meat of deer. The venison mentioned in Genesis is wild goat.

vermicelli. Few diners would want to dwell on the etymology of this word for a very thin pasta. For *vermicelli* means "little worms" in Italian, deriving from the Latin *vermis,* "worm, maggot, or crawling insect."

very poor man's dinner. An appropriate name for this Maine dish made of thinly sliced potatoes and onions fried in the grease of salt pork. A similar dish made in Massachusetts is called "Necessity Mess."

vichyssoise. The soup has a French name but was created by a chef at New York's Ritz-Carlton hotel in 1917. *Vichyssoise* means "cream soup" in French. It is specifically a cream soup of potatoes and leeks, usually served cold and garnished with chives.

vittles. Victuals, food. This backcountry southern word is actually a very old, proper English one, and *victuals* is a pedantic misspelling of it.

waffle. The waffle takes its name from the Dutch *wafel* for the crisp batter cake baked in a waffle iron. But folklore holds that it was created by a knight who had returned to England from the Crusades in 1204. Sir Giles, it is said, came into the kitchen where his wife was baking cakes and accidentally sat on one while wearing his full suit of chain armor. He smashed the cake flat as a pancake but with rows of little indentations—the imprint of his armor. These proved excellent for holding butter and syrup and the waffle was born. According to this tongue-in-cheek story, the delectable dish was called the waffle "because waffle is a word that is easy to pronounce when one's mouth is full!"

watercress. Both watercress and land cress are herbs of the mustard group. Cress takes its name from the German *kresse,* for the salad green, this word perhaps deriving from an older German word that meant "to creep or crawl" and described the plant's way of growing.

watermelon. Originating in Africa, watermelon has been cultivated for thousands of years, but seems to have been so named only since 1605. There were many old names for the melon, including names in Arabic and Sanskrit. The watermelon is an important water source in many arid regions but considered a fruit dessert in most places. Mark Twain considered it "chief of the world's luxuries ... When one has tasted it, he knows what angels eat." The Chinese call the watermelon the *west-melon* (shih-quah).

western sandwich. A sandwich made of an omelet with onions, green peppers, and chopped ham between slices of bread or toast; also called a *Denver sandwich.*

What am I, chopped liver? A half-humorous complaint that a person is being regarded as trivial or unimportant. The phrase was first recorded in a routine of American comedian Jimmy Durante.

Where's the beef? Actress Clara Peller delivered this line hundreds of times in a 1984 television ad campaign for the Wendy's hamburger chain comparing the beef content of its burgers with that of its competitors. The words soon became a catchphrase meaning "where's the real substance of a plan, or an idea, or an issue." It is still heard, often in political circles, as when Walter Mondale used it in his unsuccessful run for president in 1984.

whiskey. *Whiskey,* first recorded in 1715, is the spelling used by the Irish, Americans, and French, while the English spell the stuff *whisky,* as do the Germans. Call for whiskey in almost any country in the world and you'll get what you want—a truly universal word that is an Anglicized version of the Gaelic *uisce beathadh,* "water of life." *See* MARTINI.

the whiskey is all right but the meat is weak. Computers will never take the place of human translators, as the above illustrates. It is said to have been produced recently by an electronic translator as a translation of *the spirit is willing but the flesh is weak*!

white bread. Relatively recent slang, white-bread means "bland," or "white middle-class values." It goes back to the 1970s, first recorded in 1977, when *Newsweek* reported that a top black comedian walked off a Las Vegas stage "fed up with doing white bread humor." The expression may have black origins, but this is not certain. It may also be partly a pun of *white-bred,* but it mostly refers to the synthetic white bread of the supermarket, without flavor or character.

white meat. A Victorian term still often used in America for the breast meat of a chicken or turkey, which the British call breast. "May I have some breast?" Winston Churchill once asked his American hostess at a buffet luncheon. "In this country, Mr. Churchill, we say *white meat* or *dark meat,*" his hostess replied, a little prissily. Churchill apologized and the next day sent her an orchid along with a card reading, "I would be most obliged if you would pin this on your white meat." *White meat* and *dark meat* are also derogatory slang terms applied to white or black men and women, usually in a sexual sense.

wild pork. Bear meat. According to an old recipe the way to cook wild pork (a slang term for bear meat) is drop several hot rocks in a pot of boiling water with the meat for several hours. Then, throw the meat away and eat the rocks.

William Tell's apple. According to fable, William Tell was a famous marksman and the champion of Swiss Independence when Switzerland was ruled by Austria in the 13th century. Tell refused to salute the imperial governor and was sentenced to shoot an apple from his son's head. After doing this, another arrow fell from his coat and the governor demanded to know what it had been intended for. "To shoot you with, had I failed in the task imposed upon me," Tell told him and he was cast in prison, from which he was rescued and went on to lead his country to freedom. There are at least 10 earlier versions of the tale involving other countries and heroes, the oldest found in the Old Norse *Vilkinia Saga.*

wine book. According to an October 31, 1989 article in the *New York Times,* a wine book is a ledger in which the crew leaders or bosses of migrant workers "record the claims that they make on the worker's wages, beyond the $40 or $50 per week that they charge for their meals. The name of a worker is written at the top of each page, which, except for the occasional date and odd notation is nothing but a list of numbers showing dollars and cents. But the crew leaders know what transaction each charge represents." Transactions often include wine, of course, and also cocaine and crack, the crew leaders rarely telling a worker the high price of the drugs until the money is deducted from his salary. Such are the more subtle ways of debt servitude today. The expression *wine book* has been around at least two or three decades but is not often recorded.

wine of ape. Surly or obnoxious drunkenness. Brewer tells us: "There is a Talmud parable which says that Satan came one day to drink with Noah, and slew a lamb, a lion, a pig, and an ape, to teach Noah that man before wine is in him is a lamb, when he drinks moderately he is a lion, when like a sot he is a swine, but after that any further excess makes him an ape that senselessly chatters and jabbers." Other sources say Satan killed and buried the animals near vines Noah was planting. Why Satan would give Noah any advice is not explained.

the world is my oyster. All the pleasures and opportunities of life are open to someone because he is young, rich, handsome, successful, etc. Shakespeare invented or popularized this expression in *The Merry Wives of Windsor* (1600): *Falstaff:* I will not lend thee a penny. Pistol: Why, then, the world's mine oyster which I with sword will open.

Y

yam. *Yam* can be traced back to the Senegal *nyami,* meaning "to eat," and was introduced to America via the Gullah dialect *njam,* meaning the same, in 1676. The word, however, had come into European use long before this.

yes, we have no bananas. Originally, this was the title of a song written by Americans Frank Silver and Irving Cohen in 1923. One story has the team borrowing the first line from wordsmith Tad Dorgan and creating the song with the refrain "Yes, we have no bananas, / We have no bananas today." Another more dramatic account has Silver getting the idea for the song when he heard a Greek fruit peddler yell up to a woman at a New York City tenement window, "Yes, we have no bananas!" Whatever the case, the song became immensely popular, and, according to H. L. Mencken, *yes, we have no bananas* became the most widely used catchphrase of the 1920s, even spreading across the sea to England. In his book *The Illiterate Digest* (1924) Will Rogers wrote, "I would rather have been the Author of that Banana Masterpiece than the author of the Constitution of the United States."

Yorkshire pudding. Not a dessert pudding, but an unsweetened baked batter made of flour, salt, eggs, and milk that is often put under roasting meat to catch its drippings. *Yorkshire pudding* honors the county in northern England where it was invented or perfected, its name being first recorded in a 1747 cookbook.

you can't have your cake and eat it too. An old saying recorded in John Heywood's *The Proverbes of John Heywood* (1546) It was originally: *Would you both eat your cake and have your cake?*

you can't make an omelet without breaking eggs. The end justifies the means; sometimes evil must be done to accomplish good. Russian communist leader V. I. Lenin is said to have originated the saying, though this is far from certain.

youngberry. The youngberry is generally considered to be a hybrid variety of dewberry, which, in turn, is simply an early-ripening prostrate form of blackberry. The large, dark purple sweet fruit has the high aroma and flavor of the loganberry and native blackberry. The youngberry was developed by Louisiana horticulturist B. M. Young about 1900 by crossing a southern dewberry and trailing blackberry, or several varieties of blackberries. Its long, trailing canes are generally trained on wires. Popular in the home garden, the berry is extensively planted in the American Southwest, South, Pacific Northwest, and California.

ziti. Familiar to Americans in the form of the tasty Italian dish baked ziti, the word *ziti* is the name of a tubular pasta that derives from the obsolete Italian word *ziti,* meaning "boys." The phallic shape of the pasta may have suggested the "boys" appellation.

zwieback. Zwieback is a hard dry toast popular with adults and even made specifically for babies. The word, first recorded here in 1894, is a German one meaning "twice baked."